My Sisters' Prayers to Our Father
Devotional

My Sisters' Prayers to Our Father

Copyright © 2024 by Dr. Dana E. Neal and Sisters

Scriptures are taken from various sources, i.e. the *Authorized King James Version, New King James Version, NLT, NIV, CSB, and Message Bibles*

Revised Edition
Edited by: Solutions 4 You
Cover Designed by: Tiffany Kreations and Miss Danisha via Canva

Printed in the United States of America

Published by:
Dana Elaine Ministries

My Sisters' Prayers to Our Father

Devotional

Dr. Dana Elaine and Sisters

Dedication

"Likewise the Spirit also helpeth our infirmities: for we know not what we should pray for as we ought: but the Spirit itself maketh intercession for us with groanings which cannot be uttered. [27] And He that searcheth the hearts knoweth what is the mind of the Spirit, because He maketh intercession for the saints according to the will of God."

This book is dedicated to the precious Holy Spirit Who helps us to pray according to Romans 8:26-27. Truly the Holy Spirit's help was needed to pray the various topics and issues that are lifted up in this compilation of prayers. Holy Spirit without You leading and guiding this work, it could not have been done. You have been the help of all of us who have prayed with sincerity of heart and mind.

This book is also dedicated to all my sisters (CLC family, Prayer Everywhere partners, relatives, and friends) who answered the call to be a part of this sisters' project. Thank you for your prayers. I believe many will be blessed as they delve into this devotional, praying the prayers of faith in partnership with you and the Holy Spirit. Thank you again.

Finally, this book is dedicated to all who end up with this book in their hands and pray the prayers of faith. We touch and agree with you in prayer. May the Lord hear you when you call, and may you see answered prayers!

Dr. Dana Elaine

Table of Contents

Acknowledgements

I would like to first acknowledge my Lord and Savior Jesus Christ. My relationship with Him draws me into a posture of prayer. He asked His disciples, could they not have prayed with Him for one hour? That question alone, provokes me to pray and I thank Him for the sweet hour of prayer. The time I am able to spend with the Father, the Son and the Holy Spirit is invaluable. Lord, I pray because of You and in Your name. I acknowledge and thank God the Father Who has given me access to come before His throne and Who hears and answers even my faintest cry. I acknowledge the Holy Spirit Who makes intercessions and groanings I cannot utter. He is my great Intercessor and Prayer Partner.

I want to acknowledge the praying people in my life, beginning with my late grandmother, Queen Ballard. She taught me from a child to pray and to pray without ceasing. Although her prayers were so loud that they could be heard out of our house windows into the streets, and were quite embarrassing for me as a child, they have undoubtedly shaped my prayer life today. I understand now that those prayers covered our household. It is because of grandma's prayers that she, my mother, my five siblings and I, as well as others who came across our threshold, were protected and covered under the blood of Jesus. I acknowledge and thank my mom who has taken the torch and prays without ceasing for her children, grandchildren, great grandchildren, and others that God lays upon her heart. I acknowledge and thank Bishop Teal and Prayer Everywhere for reminding us daily, 365 days a year, to keep prayer primary in our Christian walk and to take prayer everywhere.

Last, but certainly not least, I acknowledge my children who are my inspiration; who always encourage me to do more because they believe in me. Thank you! And, thank you Danisha and Tiffany for helping me with this project. Ladies, you were a tremendous help in the huge undertaking of bringing this vision to pass. I am tremendously grateful! Your assistance was much needed and a godsend! Wendell, your checking on my progress was enough! Love you all.

Dr. Dana Elaine

Preface

The sisters of "My Sisters' Prayers to Our Father" invite you on a journey of prayer with us. We want you to come alongside us as we come alongside you to intercede for each other, our loved ones, our nation, and many other cares and concerns that rest upon our hearts. The scripture tells us that we can cast our cares upon the Lord because He cares for us. Let's cast our cares together. We are your prayer partners. Most importantly, the Holy Spirit is your Prayer Partner Who will lead and guide you in your prayer time. Hear the deep calling to the deep, and prepare to have some conversations with the Father..

Although this book of prayers is a collaborative effort of sisters in Christ, this is still your personal devotional time with God. Go in your prayer closet, shut the door, and let your request be made known unto the Father. Be confident when you pray that He hears you whether you are crying out for yourself or for someone else, or for your child or for someone else's child. He hears you whether you are crying out for your household, your marriage, your family, or the entire nation. So get in your posture of prayer, book in hand, and pray these prayers day by day, page by page, and prayer by prayer. There is always a reason to pray. There is always someone to pray for or something to pray about. And I decree and declare that when you pray, the Lord will hear and He will answer. Believe to see results!

Also, included between the pages of this book is space behind each prayer for you to write your own prayer. This will allow you to tell God exactly what is on your heart and mind, and give you more time to spend in God's presence, soaking in His love. So, enjoy!

Pray the prayers and believe when you pray that you are making a difference!

The Father is waiting to hear from you.

"Humble yourselves therefore under the mighty hand of God, that He may exalt you in due time: Casting all your care upon Him; for He careth for you." (1 Peter 5:6-7)

Opening
Prayer of Praise

"I will bless the LORD at all times: His praise shall continually be in my mouth."

Psalm 34:1

Dear graciously heavenly Father, before Your daughters ask You for anything, we just wanted to praise and bless You for everything! You are a good, good Father and we give You praise for Who You are to us. We honor You Father, and cast every accolade at Your feet.

Father God, You are majestic in all of Your ways and there is none like You! Your glory spans across the skies and the seas; the mountains and the meadows; the atmosphere and stratosphere; the hemisphere and the heavens. You are clothed in majesty, splendor, and power. You are altogether lovely. There is none like You. You are God and beside You there is no other. We honor You in all of Your ways. We praise You for Who You are. You are more than enough. You are more than life itself. You are more than what our minds could ever comprehend. You are high and lofty, yet low and loving. How great are You God! You are greater than great. Better than better. Simply breath taking! Esteemed above all else.

Lord, we praise You; we adore You. You are Alpha and Omega, the Beginning and the End, the First and the Last. You are everything from A to Z and everything in between. Who can compare to You? There is no God like Jehovah, our God. You have no rival and You have no equal. You created the heavens and the earth. You flung the stars in the sky, put the fish in the seas, and the cattle in the fields. You created man and made him a living soul. You are God! The earth is Yours Lord and the fullness thereof, and all that dwell therein. You founded it upon the seas and established it upon the floods. We are Your people and the sheep of Your pasture. We bow down and give You praise, honor and adoration. We lie prostrate in Your presence. We weep at Your feet, washing them with our tears, and drying them with our hair. We join the heavenly host of angels to worship You. The angels bow before You and heaven and earth adore You. You are God! Hallelujah! Your glory fills the earth.

God, You make our joy complete! You satisfy the longing of our souls and quench our thirst. We drink from Your well and we thirst no more. From the rising of the sun, until the going down of the same, You are worthy to be praised. Father, we laude our praises upon You. You have been so good to us. You have been our help and our hope, our husband, Father, and friend. You have been our promise keeper, protector and provider; our lover and the lifter of our heads. You have been our Comforter and our courage. Our hearts beat after You, oh Lord. Be lifted up! Be praised! Be glorified! Be exalted! You are our God and our King! Let our praises go before Your throne as a sweet aroma in Your nostrils. It is in the precious name of Jesus we pray, amen.

Dr. Dana Elaine
Dana Elaine Ministries
Baltimore, MD

A Closer Walk with God

*"When thou saidst, Seek ye My face; my heart said unto Thee, Thy
face, Lord will I seek."*

Psalm 27:8

God, You declare in Your Word, *"If my people, which are called by
my name, shall humble themselves, and pray, and seek My face, and
turn from their wicked ways; then will I hear from heaven, and will
forgive their sin, and will heal their land."* (2 Chronicles 7:14). Lord, I
will seek You with my whole heart—in times of worship, prayer,
fasting, and studying Your Word. Your face Lord will I seek. Being in
Your presence is not an option for me. It is a necessity. You are the
very breath that I breathe: my Ruach, my source, and my strength.

God, I am glad to know that no matter where I go, You are there.
*"For where shall I go from Thy spirit? Or where shall I flee from Thy
presence? If I ascend up into heaven, Thou art there: if I make my
bed in hell, behold, Thou art there. If I take the wings of the
morning, and dwell in the uttermost parts of the sea; even there
shall Thy hand lead me, and Thy right hand shall hold me."*
(Psalm139:7-10). How could I not reverence and worship You? You
leave no stone unturned concerning me! There is no place that You
would not go to be near me. When I feel all alone, isolated and
abandoned, there You are God! When it seems like there is no one
to support me, there You are, my Advocator. When it seems like
there is no one to encourage me or just sit with me, there You are
Lord, my Comforter. You know where to find me. Your Word is true.

You will never leave nor forsake me. No matter where I am, You are there! You are there to feel my joy and my pain. You are close enough to hear my cry. You uphold me. There is no place I can go without Your presence. That brings me great joy and a great sense of security.

Continue to be near me Lord. Continue to draw me into Your presence so that I may see and declare Your great and mighty works. I stand in awe of You! You have been and continue to be my dwelling place and place of refuge. I love being near You. I love being in Your presence. Even now, I want to get closer. Draw me closer. How close can I get to You Lord? You are the Lover of my soul. A closer walk is my heart's desire. Pull me away from every distraction and draw me into Your presence. Let me rest my head on Your breast; let me be ever so near. Thank You Lord for this closeness we share.

My Righteous Redeemer, the One Who saves is near to me. Wherever I go, You are there. How comforting to my soul! I will hold on to this truth. When I am lonely, I will call on You. When it feels like all hope is lost, I will reach out to You. I know You will always be here for me: providing, guiding, shielding, forgiving, and loving me. I can count on You Lord. You will always be here as the health of my countenance and the lifter of my head, pushing me pass my discomforts and helping me to walk into my purpose. You are here Lord moving in my life, giving me a testimony and a praise. I will keep seeking Your face, desiring Your presence and singing...

Just a closer walk with thee; grant it Jesus if You please.
Daily walking close to thee; let it be, dear Lord.
Let it be! (Ella Fitzgerald_)

In Jesus' name. Amen!

Reverend Patricia Levi
Christian Life Church
Baltimore, MD

Dear Father,

_____

_____

_____

_____

_____

_____

_____

_____

_____

_____

_____

Inspirational Thought:

God is only a breath away. Breathe in and experience His nearness, experience His love.

Draw Us Closer Lord

"The Lord is my shepherd; I shall not want. He maketh me to lie down in green pastures: He leadeth me beside the still waters. He restoreth my soul: He leadeth me in the paths of righteousness for His name's sake. Yea, though I walk through the valley of the shadow of death, I will fear no evil: for Thou art with me; Thy rod and Thy staff they comfort me. Thou preparest a table before me in the presence of mine enemies: Thou anointest my head with oil; my cup runneth over. Surely goodness and mercy shall follow me all the days of my life: and I will dwell in the house of the Lord for ever."

Psalm 23

Dear heavenly Father, in the mighty name of Jesus we come before Your throne giving You all the glory, all the honor, and all the praise for Who You are to us. We thank You for being Jehovah Jireh our Provider and Jehovah Nissi, our Banner (our protection and victory in the battle). We depend totally upon You from day to day, minute by minute.

Dear God, as we travel through this life, we desire a closer walk with You. We realize that we cannot make it without You. We need You in every way. We need to know You are near, close by, just a prayer away. Please bless us with discernment so that we will be able to hear and recognize Your voice clearly and be confident that You are guiding us in the way we should go. We ask You Lord to order our steps in every situation that we may encounter so that we will always be in Your will.

Be in the midst of Your people God, whether in a crowded room or in our time of solitude. We long to be close to You and experience Your perfect peace. We yearn for Your presence on a daily basis for You promised to never leave us alone. We thank You for keeping us in Your care and blessing us with new mercies every morning. Your love is essential for us to make it through this Christian journey. Thank You for surrounding us with Your love and drawing us closer.

Father God, thank You for Your Word that draws us closer to You. Your Word is our anchor. It sustains us. Let Your Word be a lamp unto our feet and a light unto our path. Let it be hidden in our hearts so we will not sin against You. We thank You for Your Word and for the Holy Spirit Who guides us and dwells within us. We want all of You. Draw us in; never let us go. Let us feel Your presence both night and day. Keep us ever so close. In the mighty name of Jesus we pray, amen.

Tamera R. Brunson
Wayland Baptist Church
Baltimore, MD

My Personal Prayer to Be Closer to God

Dear Father,

_____

_____

_____

_____

_____

_____

_____

_____

_____

_____

Inspirational Thought:

"The Lord is near to all who call upon Him, to all who call upon Him in truth." (Psalm 145:18). Never think God is far from you. Just call on Him. He is closer than you think, and ready to hear and ready to save.

Walking in God's Purpose

"The Lord will fulfill His purpose for me; Your steadfast love, O Lord endures forever."

Psalm 138:8

Everlasting Father, Wonderful Counselor, Mighty God, how great are You Lord in all the earth! You have created the heavens and the earth and by You all things were made! I thank You that even before we were formed in our mothers' wombs You knew us and had already mapped out a sure plan for our lives. Your plan, purpose, and will for us are perfect. We could have never designed a more perfect plan for Your thoughts are higher than our thoughts and Your ways higher than our ways. You are the all seeing, all knowing, all wise God!

Now, Lord, I pray You will give me and my sisters clarity and reveal Your purpose and plan for our lives. Reveal our spiritual gifts, those You uniquely designed for each of us to use for Your glory. Help us to be obedient to Your voice as we endeavor to fulfill our God given purpose. Father, we pray for guidance and direction according to Your Word that says, *"If you need wisdom, ask our generous God, and He will give it to you. He will not rebuke you for asking"*. (James 1:5). Give us Your divine wisdom as we begin to take faith-filled steps toward knowing and walking in Your purpose. Grant us passion and persistence to pursue You daily. Enable and equip us to exhaust every gift and talent You have given us to glorify Your name. Prompt us if we begin to get side tracked or stagnated. Take charge of our eyes, ears, hearts and minds, and order our steps! Teach us to be confident in our pursuit of what You have called us to do, to be and to have. God, help us to keep our motives pure, with our only intent being to be a servant of Christ and not a pleaser of man. As we walk in our purpose, help us to keep the testimony of our brother Paul who begs the question and then answers it in Galatians 1:10, *"Am I now trying to win the approval of human beings, or of God? Or am I trying to please people? If I were still trying to please people, I would not be a servant of Christ."* Lord, we do not wish to please people or seek to gain their approval. But our hearts' desire is to find favor with You in our service to others. We want Your approval in all that we do.

God, You said in Your Word that You chose us and appointed us to go and bear fruit. So, Lord let Your will and purpose be manifested in our lives so that we can bear the fruit You expect from each of us. God, we pray for divine connections and opportunities that will inspire, uplift, and confirm what You are doing in our lives. God, thank You for opening doors that only You can open and no man can shut. And then Lord, thank You for shutting doors in our lives that You never intended to be opened. We want to be in Your will, doing mighty things for You. We know it is possible because Your Word says You are *"...able to do exceedingly, abundantly, above all that we ask or think, according to the power that works in us."* (Ephesians 3:20). Father, we commit every area of our lives to You to do Your will and Your good pleasure. God give us the clarity that we need. Give us the wisdom that we need. Give us divine revelation. And then Lord, give us sudden activation! Let us get on the move for You! No more delay! Let Your power in us be manifested in the earth as we walk in our God given assignments. Do exceedingly and abundantly!

Father, we pray for Your peace and Your covering as we courageously make the decision to step out and walk in our purpose. Please work on our behalf as we continue to surrender our lives to You. God, we pray against every plan of the enemy that is designed to distract, discourage, or disrupt our God-given purpose! We bind up anxiety, fears, and doubts that would try to hinder us or weigh us down. Through our prayer and our faith, we know that even now you are releasing Your Power in our lives to accomplish Your will. We move forward, not in fear, but with love, power, and a sound mind. May You be glorified in all that we do and say. Thank You for choosing us! In Jesus' name, amen.

Sister LaSandra Jackson
Mt. Pleasant Church and Ministries
Baltimore, MD

My Personal Prayer to Walk in God's Purpose

Dear Father,

_____

_____

_____

_____

_____

_____

_____

_____

_____

_____

Inspirational Thought:

God has a divine purpose for your life. You are His handiwork, created in Christ to do good works. Seek to do the will of God Who has sent you in the earth for such a time as this.

Prayer for God's Love to be Known

"And I pray that you, being rooted and established in love, may have power, together with all the Lord's holy people, to grasp how wide and long and high and deep is the love of Christ, and to know this love that surpasses knowledge—that you may be filled to the measure of all the fullness of God."
Ephesians 3: 17-19

Dear Heavenly Father, thank You for Your love. You are love and Your love will never fail. Thank You for the moments You create for us to feel Your love. We feel love in the warmth of our families and through the love of our friends. We feel love in those precious moments and beautiful settings we share with our loved ones and so appreciate. And Father, even still, we esteem Your love far above all else. Your love runs deeper and wider than human love. It is self-less and sacrificial. It is unwavering and unyielding. It is everlasting. It exemplifies Your very character. Teach us to know You Lord, to know Your love. Let Your love be known to the church and to the world. Open up the eyes of our understanding so that Your love will be appreciated and embraced by all. Your love is so great. We should all know the depths of this kind of love. You showed Your great love to the world by sending Jesus to die for us that we might live. Lord, You showed Your love on the night You were betrayed and You washed the feet of Your disciples, including the one who would betray You. You showed love when You gave Your life for all humanity, shedding Your precious blood for the remission of our sins. Jesus, Your love for us took You to the cross to die for us. Because of Your love, our broken fellowship with the Father has been restored. What love!

Then God, we see Your great love in the gift of the precious Holy Spirit. He is here, moving about the earth, available to all to be our Comforter, our Keeper, our Help, our Guide, and so much more! Your love is shed abroad! It is disbursed widely to all mankind. I pray it be known throughout the world so many will come proclaiming, "What manner of love! What must I do to be saved?"

Father, help us to take full advantage of the benefits of Your love toward us. Your love gives us hope. Your love makes us unashamed. It clears our guilt and our guilty conscious. Your love is patient, kind and longsuffering. It does not retaliate against others. It does not boast itself in pride. It is genuine. It is active. It is righteous and it is true. Lord, we thank You for this amazing kind of love. Let Your love be known in all the earth.

I pray the world recognizes Your love in every sunrise and in every sunset, in every rainfall and in every ocean's wave, in every winter and in every summer—in all that surrounds us. Remind us that Your creation bears witness of Your love. Open our eyes and teach us Lord. Reveal Your truth to our hearts concerning Your love. Let Your love be known not only through sunsets and sunrises, but through Your people. Help us to operate in love, showing it, as You have shown it to us. You have loved us and do love us each day. Teach us to love one another in like manner as Your Word has commanded. Lord, in ourselves, we do not know how to love. We need the help of Your Holy Spirit. Fill us with Your Spirit of love so that we can lay down our pride and our beautiful garments to take up our servant's cloth and wash one another's feet. Lord, let Your love be known through us, seen through us, and felt through us. Lord, let us love freely as You have freely loved us.

Love judges equitably. Love picks up the fallen. Love heals the broken. Love speaks words that even the blind can see and the deaf can hear. Lord, let Your love be known. Let Your love be communicated. Let Your love be received.

Finally, dear God, Your love is our present help. It is a faith builder and a fear destroyer for *"...perfect love casteth out fear."* (1 John 4:18). When we know this love, we can face our enemies and slay our giants. We can endure tests and trials and get through grief, hardship, and pain. Your love brings peace to our heart. God, we trust Your love. Let it be known in all the earth. In Jesus mighty name, we pray. Amen.

Sister Susan K. Leeks
Christian Life Church
Baltimore, MD

My Personal Prayer to Know God's Love

Dear Father,

_____

_____

_____

_____

_____

_____

_____

_____

_____

_____

Inspirational Thought:

Remember, God loves you. Be free to love others. *"A new command I give you: Love one another. As I have loved you, so you must love one another. By this everyone will know that you are My disciples, if you love one another."* John 13:34-35

God's Love Revealed

"We love because He first loved us. If anyone says, "I love God,"
and hates his brother, he is a liar; for he who does not love his
brother whom he has seen cannot love God Whom he has not
seen. And this commandment we have from Him: whoever loves
God must also love his brother."
1 John 4:19-21

Dear Jesus, I give honor and glory to Your name. I humbly come to You on bended knees and opened arms to receive Your love for me. Your love is faithful and true. It is graceful, merciful, forgiving, eternal, unconditional, and so much more than I can conceive. Lord, let me see through Your eyes to witness Your merciful, loving gaze upon Your people. I want to see others as You see them so that I can love them with Your love. Speak to me oh Lord. Whisper in my ears Your truth about my purpose to serve You by serving others in love. God, help me to fully embrace Your love so that I can give that love liberally to others.

Let Your love be seen through me and known by each person I encounter. By Your grace, open my heart and my hands to freely give to those who are homeless, hungry and in need. Help me to minister in love to their physical needs and to their spiritual needs. Empower me to courageously share the Gospel of Jesus Christ to those who are lost so that they might be saved. Lord, let me show forth Your love, Your kindness, and Your forgiveness in the land.

Then Father, when I am gripped with fear because of all the evil and wickedness in the world, give me that eternal armor of God's love to wear in the midst of my fright for Your perfect love casts out all fear. And, when my spirit is weary and worn and I need to feel Your love, let me feel the breath of Your love breathing inside me, occupying my very being. Through my struggles and pain, show me Your unconditional love that You have for me. When life becomes overwhelmingly hard, and I am heavy burdened, and the tears flow from my eyes, take me in Your loving arms and hold me tight. Let me know dear God, everything will be alright. When I am lonely, confused, and abused by those who I thought loved me, rescue me with Your love. When I am worried about the day and all of its challenges I have to face, rescue me with Your love.

Dear God, place me in the palm of Your hand, that safe place, that reassuring place that comforts my soul. Let me feel my Father's love. When all I see and hear around me is hatred and violence, wars and rumors of wars, let Your love for me be my anchor. Let Your love ground me and settle my heart so I will not be shaken. I must endure so others can see how Your love rescues and saves.

Lord, Your love compels me. It makes me want to know even more about Your love. I pray for an awakening. Open up my understanding to Your love and Your compassion. Somebody needs to see Your love through me, dear Lord. Revive my soul so that I may be used for Your glory.

"The true awakening of my soul to do Thy will I wish to behold. Then God, at the end of my day, when I am stressed and restless from all that I endured, let Your love be my lullaby. During my sleepless nights, let the angels sing over me melodies of peace, calm and tranquility to put my mind at rest and let me sleep. Refresh me Lord

with Your love. Let me hear You call my name, telling me all is well as I lay on my bed. Let Your love turn my sleepless nights in a time of divine rest for my body and soul. "

Dear God, I thank You for revealing Your love to me as a sweet aroma. I have received richly from Your love and will freely give the same to others. Let us all receive Your love God, and let us all radiate with the Light of Your glory! In Jesus mighty name I pray. Amen.

Sister Wanda Brewton
Prayer for the Children
Baltimore, MD

Dear Father,

_____

_____

_____

_____

_____

_____

_____

_____

Inspirational Thought:

If you do not know anything else, know that God loves you. That is a fact and you cannot change it. Your shortcomings and failures do not stifle God's love for you. His love is unconditional. So when you doubt the love of God, remember He is love and it is impossible for Him not to love. *"So we have come to know and to believe the love that God has for us. God is love, and whoever abides in love abides in God, and God abides in him."* 1 John 4:16

Salvation for the Lost

"The Lord is not slack concerning His promise, as some men count slackness; but is longsuffering toward us, not willing that any should perish but that all should come to repentance."

2 Peter 3:9

Father God, we honor You. We humbly bow down before Your presence, blessing and praising Your Holy name. Thank You for being the giver of life and making a way for fallen man. We were born in sin and shaped in iniquity and there is nothing we can do on our own to rectify our wrong. Thank You God that by Your tender mercies, You made provision for us to be in a right relationship with You. You did for us what we could not do for ourselves. Thank You for Your love! You desire that none would be lost, none would perish; but that all would repent and come to the salvation knowledge of Jesus Christ. That is why we lift our voices to You today. We pray that the lost would be saved, delivered, and set free from their sins.

Father, according to Your Word, the harvest is plenteous but the laborers are few. Please send forth laborers into the harvest to share the Gospel of Jesus Christ so that souls might be saved. God, we know the way has already been made to save the lost. You loved us so much that You gave us Your only begotten son Jesus to be our Redeemer and Savior. He paid the full penalty for the sins of mankind. He suffered and died on an old rugged cross on Calvary

Hill, and You raised Him back to life on the third day with all power in His hand. He has the power to save us from our sins, to make us alive again, and to bring us into an eternal relationship with You. You said in Your Word that if any man be in Christ, he is a new creation. Thank You for transforming our hearts of stone and giving us hearts of flesh, making us new. Thank You for filling us with Your love and Your precious Spirit. It is a privilege and an honor to be saved! Thank You for the abundant life we have in Christ Jesus.

Father, we now commit into Your hands those who do not know You as Lord and Savior. Draw them with Your cords of love so they will desire a relationship with You through Your Son Jesus. God change them from the inside out by Your Holy Word and by the power of Your Holy Spirit! Intervene in their lives and save them from their sins by Your saving grace. Help them to yield to the prompting of the Holy Spirit and to accept You as their Lord and Savior. Be Lord and King and the head of their lives.

Father, forgive us all for trying to be masters of our own lives and attempting to live apart from You. Jesus, we know that You are the Son of God and that You are God. You came into this world to show us the way to live and to provide eternal life to all who will accept You. For as many that will receive You, You will give them the power to become the sons of God. Thank You God that I have received You. You are mine and I am Yours. Now draw others. Draw them by Your Spirit and bring them into this rich relationship with the Father, Son, and Holy Ghost. This is my humble prayer. Thank You God!

Now God, hear the prayer of the person who prays this prayer of salvation. Thank you for answering them and saving their soul today. In Jesus' name I pray, amen.

Note to the reader: If you have not accepted the Lord Jesus Christ as your Savior and want to accept Him and be saved from your sins and made a child of God, repeat the prayer below and believe in your heart the things that you pray.

"Dear God, I know that I am a sinner and cannot save myself. I believe that You love me and You desire to save my soul. I believe in my heart and confess with my mouth that You sent Your Son, Jesus to die on the cross for my sins and to give me the free gift of eternal life. Wash my sins away with the shed blood of Jesus, and come into my heart and change my life. I receive Jesus as my Lord and Savior. God, I receive all of You and I give You all of me. Take my life and make me who You would have me to be. Thank You for saving me, and for giving me eternal life as You promised in Your Word. In the name of Jesus I pray, amen."

Note to the reader: If you are reading this prayer and are unsure of your relationship with God, pray this prayer:

"Dear God, You said in Your Word that these things You have written so that we may KNOW we have eternal life and that this life is in Your Son Jesus. God I have repented of my sin and acknowledged Christ as my LORD and Savior. Therefore, based upon Your Word, I have the absolute assurance of my salvation. I am saved and I know I am saved! In the name of Jesus I pray, amen.

Senior Life Pastor May L. Henderson
The House of Prayer Everywhere
Oakland, CA

My Personal Prayer for Salvation for the Lost

Dear Father,

_____

_____

_____

_____

_____

_____

_____

_____

_____

Inspirational Thought:

Do not give up on your loved ones. God did not give up on you. Continue to pray for their salvation. No one is out of God's reach. He is just looking for someone to stand in the gap and make up the edge.

Anxiety and Worry

"Be anxious for nothing, but in everything by prayer and supplication, with thanksgiving, let your requests be made known to God; And the peace of God, which surpasses all understanding, will guard your hearts and minds through Christ Jesus."
Philippians 4:6-7

Heavenly Father, You are my Lord and my GOD, the Creator and giver of life. You created me in Your image and in Your likeness. Through Your Son Jesus Christ, and by Your Spirit, You have purchased my redemption. You have adopted me into Your royal family and made me Your daughter by which I can cry, "Abba, Father!" What a privilege! Just the thought of Who You are to me ought to take away all my worries and give me peace, for You are the God of Peace, Jehovah Shalom! But, yet, I find myself still wrestling and riddled with anxiety and worry.

Lord, I come before You now repenting and asking Your forgiveness. Forgive me for not completely trusting in You and allowing Your peace to rule my heart in troublesome times. I confess Lord, when times get difficult and life is overwhelming, and when I pray to You, I still find myself worrying and feeling uneasy about my future. My anxious thoughts run wild and anxiety seeks to overtake me. I battle within and the enemy of anxiety and worry grips my soul. I am bombarded with anxious thoughts, fear and worry. I feel imprisoned by my own thoughts of worry and fear. I must break free! Your promises await me. By Your help, I will not stay in the grips of the enemy, paralyzed with fear. Too much awaits me. I must do Your will. Lord, help me to rest in this truth—You are bigger than anything I may go through and You can handle all my stuff, big or small. You rule! You reign! You have dominion in the earth!

So today Lord, as Your Word has admonished me, I cast all my cares upon You. I cast my problems, my burdens, my worries, and my fears down at Your feet and I walk away knowing You will make everything alright. God, I thank You for being here with me, working all things together for my good. As I embrace that thought, You being here, working things out for me, it alleviates my fears and soothes my doubts. It gives me peace. You are with me. How sweet the sound! You are always by my side. It is written in Your Word that You will never leave nor forsake me. This gives me peace.

So, today Father, I make a conscious choice not to allow anxiety or worry rule over me, forfeiting my peace. I declare today, this day, the God of peace is with me and anxiety and worry are far from me! I will see them no more! My enemy, the very thing that torments me, is drowned in the Red Sea! I AM COVERED UNDER THE BLOOD OF JESUS CHRIST! I have the assurance in Your Word that I do not have to be anxious or worried about anything. But, in every situation by prayer and supplication, I can make my request known unto You, God and You will move on my behalf. So here I am Father. I give You those things I do not understand, things that make me afraid, and cause me worry and concern. I give them all to You. I lean not to my own understanding; but, in all my ways I acknowledge You, believing You will direct my path. Your peace goes far beyond my understanding. But, I will learn to live in Your peace that will guard my heart in every situation through Jesus Christ my Lord.

Abba Father, Jehovah Shalom, my Peace, this is Who You are to me. I embrace this truth. How wonderful! What a delightful feeling! I am forever grateful to You for covering and protecting my heart and mind. Anxiety and worry no longer rules my life. I declare this day, I am delivered and made whole in You! You have broken worry and anxious thoughts from off of my mind, and have rendered them powerless and useless in my life. Thank You! They no longer plague me. I dwell safely in You. My heart and mind are at ease. My soul is at rest. I am not worried, fearful, or anxious. I have been set free. Your presence is all around me. Thank You, Father. In Jesus' name, amen.

Minister Felicha F. Sinclair
Fayettsville, NC

My Personal Prayer against Anxiety and Worry

Dear Father,

_____

_____

_____

_____

_____

_____

_____

_____

_____

_____

_____

_____

Inspirational Thought:

God still sits on the throne. He is not shaken or moved. He is very much in control. You do not have to worry or be anxious. Your heavenly Father got this! Relax.

Encouragement for the Discouraged

"The Lord Himself goes before you and will be with you; He will never leave you nor forsake you. Do not be afraid; do not be discouraged."
Deuteronomy 31:8

Oh, Heavenly Father, I come humbly to Your throne of grace. I thank You Father, in times of trouble You have been my help. You have sent Your angels to watch over me both day and night. You have hedged me about with Your protection and Your grace and mercy. You have given me strength to endure whatever afflictions I might face. I am encouraged even in difficult times because You attend to my needs. I take comfort in knowing that whatever the enemy hurls my way, it will not destroy me because You have me covered on every side. I rest easy knowing that even when the world is shaken all around me, You are still seated on the throne, very much in control, working everything out for my good.

So, Father, in times of despair and in times of uncertainty, help me to remember I can always depend on You. Help me not to lean to my own understanding, but confidently rest in You, trusting with all of my heart that You will direct my path in a way that is best for me. I will walk before You with a pure heart of faith when facing test and trials, unwavering faith, not discouraged by what I see or what I might be going through. I am encouraged in knowing that You will walk with me and be my guide. Through my ups and my downs, You will sustain me. You will plant my feet on the solid Rock! I will be steady! I will be unmovable! I will not be shaken.

Dear Lord, I will not be overly concerned by the things I go through in this life. But I will honor You with my faith. When strong winds blow and the storm is raging all around me, I will trust in You and hold onto Your unchanging hand. You are faithful to see me through. When discouragement tries to overtake me, I will look to You for You are the lifter of my head. In those times that I become weak, I trust that You God will renew my strength, my hope, and my joy. Father, help me to remember that trouble does not last always. When my heart is overwhelmed, and fear is lurking, ready to pounce on me and bring that unsettling feeling; and when the enemy comes up against me, like a thief in the night to rob me of my peace, Lord be my banner of victory. Let me wave my banner in the midst of it all, declaring with full assurance, I GOT THE VICTORY! Sweet, sweet victory in Jesus!

I will lift up my eyes to the hills from where my help comes. It comes from You, the Maker of heaven and earth. I will hide in Your pavilion, in the secret place of Your tabernacle shall You hide me and set me upon a Rock. You are my rest when I am wearied and burdened. You are my hope when all hope is gone. I hear Your soft voice whispering in my ear, "I will never leave nor forsake you My daughter. Take courage in Me." My heart is encouraged Lord. I take courage in You. I surrender all to You. Thank You for delivering me from everything that stresses me and thank You for giving me peace. I will forever glorify and magnify Your name on high! In Jesus' name, amen.

Deaconess Gloria White
Israel Baptist Church
Baltimore, MD

My Personal Prayer for Encouragement

Dear Father,

_____

_____

_____

_____

_____

_____

_____

_____

_____

_____

Inspirational Thought:

If you knew how the Father loved you, that alone would be medicine for your soul and be the lifter of your head. Let God's love encourage your heart. He loves you with an everlasting love. *"Why, my soul, are you downcast? Why so disturbed within me? Put your hope in God, for I will yet praise Him, my Savior and my God."* Psalm 42:5.

Send a Revival

"If My people, who are called by My name, will humble themselves and pray and seek My face and turn from their wicked ways, then I will hear from heaven, and I will forgive their sin and will heal their land."

2 Chronicles 7:14

"...Our Father Who art in heaven, Hallowed be Thy name. Thy Kingdom come, Thy will be done, on earth as it is in heaven." (Matthew 6:9-10). Oh Lord, who is like unto You? You are glorious and wonderful. You are holy and righteous. Oh Lord, who is like unto You? You are excellent and majestic. You are full of grace and mercy. You are awesome and full of splendor. You perform great works. You alone are God and there is none like You. By Your mighty power, You have triumphed over all Your enemies. By Your mighty Word You created the heavens and the earth and all that is in them. You are Supreme over all the earth. You are Ruler, Lord, Master, Savior, and Deliverer. Please hear the cries of Your people. We are Your people and the sheep of Your pasture. You are our strength, and You are our great Redeemer. We seek Your face. Please come to our aid. Please have compassion on us.

Our world is plagued with uncertainty, fear, terror, confusion, lawlessness, pain, sorrow, suffering, chaos, worry, depression, and anxiety. It is filled with sickness, disease, panic, poverty, famine, witchcraft, dissentions, factions, rioting, hatred, anger, bitterness, immorality, and death. There are wars and rumors of wars. So much is going on in our world. We cannot even begin to name it all. Even nature has risen up against mankind with fires, floods, winds, ice, and storms. Idolatry is everywhere, and people are guilty of bowing at the altars of consumerism, materialism, power, careers, money, fame, fortune, education, and humanism. Spinning, spinning... It seems the whole earth is spinning out of control. We need Your help. You are the only One Who can save us Lord.

Oh Lord, send a great revival throughout the earth. Call Your church, the Ecclesia, from the four corners of the world to rise up and take its rightful place in You. Let us walk in the Spirit of truth, proclaiming Your Word to this lost and dying world. Breathe life on Your church and bring the dry bones together. Put tendons, flesh, and sinew on the frail frames of what we call the church and cause us to live again. God, we confess that we are a sinful people. Forgive us for our iniquities, for we have sinned and done evil in Your sight. We have offended You. We have rebelled against You. We have turned our backs on You. We have become complacent and indifferent towards You. We have bowed at the altars of the world. Please forgive us. Evil is applauded. Immorality is glorified. Right is considered wrong and wrong is considered right. We have lent ourselves to those who do wicked things. Please, please forgive us. Holy Spirit, we confess that we have become like the world and have allowed the ways of the world to inspire how we worship and how we live. Please forgive us dear Lord.

Oh Lord, raise up a Joshua and a Caleb generation that will believe everything You have said. Raise up godly, strong, and committed preachers, teachers, evangelists, pastors, and missionaries. Release Your anointing on the prayer warriors and intercessors. Restore to us the joy of our salvation. Rekindle the flame of our passion for

You. Renew our minds. Resurrect our hope. Help us to tear down the idols we have built up, idols of pride and arrogance, selfish gain, and carnality. Help us to walk humbly before Your throne. Help us to declare the Word of the Lord from the four corners of the earth. Let Your Word be lifted up in the earth.

We confess that those of faith have been lax and lazy; so, we ask that You bring us back to the place where we first believed You. We throw ourselves on Your altar and we ask for Your mercy. We plead with You to remember that we are only dust. We plead with You to cast our sins as far as the east is from the west. Blot out our transgressions, oh Lord. We need You! We are crying out to You, turning down our plates, and seeking Your will. Let the mind of Christ be our desire. Let the love of the Lord be our satisfaction. Let the zeal of the early church be our example. Fill the church buildings to overflowing with hungry souls looking to be fed and thirsty hearts wanting to be refreshed. Lord, send a revival! Let there be a great reawakening, a great move of God, and a great move of salvation, miracles, signs, and wonders.

We are Your church and the gates of hell shall not prevail against us. On Christ the solid Rock we stand. Put running in our feet that will lead us to foreign land and to foreign people to share the Good News of the Gospel of Jesus Christ. We are Your church, and we stand at attention waiting for further instructions from the throne of heaven. Thank You, Lord, for hearing our humble cry, forgiving our sins, and sending a revival in our land. In Jesus' name we pray. Amen.

Executive Pastor, Rev. Pamula Yerby-Hammack
City of Abraham Church & Ministries
Baltimore, MD

My Personal Prayer for Revival in the Land

Dear Father,

Inspirational Thought:

God desires to water our land with the dew of His Spirit—the Refreshing Springs and the Living Waters. But, our land is dry and the people are dry. Will you pray that God will saturate the land, and that we will see the greatest outpouring ever, like on the day of Pentecost!

Revive Us Oh Lord

"Then we will not turn away from You: revive us, and we will call on Your name"

Psalm 80:18

Dear Holy Father, we need a revival in our land. We need a revival in the church! We want to see the Holy Ghost power of God moving amid Your people with miracles, signs, and wonders following those who believe. Let the sick be healed, blinded eyes and deaf ears be opened, and the dead be brought back to life in Jesus' mighty name! Let the Holy Spirit saturate our lives and bring us in alignment with Your Word, Your will, and Your way. Revive us oh Lord! Send Your fire! Ignite us with passion! Cause us to rise up and go into the highways and byways to boldly compel men and women, boys and girls, to call upon Your great name. Put the fire of God under our feet and cause us to run with the Gospel of Jesus Christ like never before, sharing the Good News. Let millions of souls be saved. Let revival and restoration take place in Jesus' name!

We need a revival oh Lord! Breathe on us and revive us so that we can rebuild the temple of God and repair its ruins. Revive us so that we can get the latter glory of God back in the house of the Lord. We want to see Your fire fall down from heaven, breaking and destroying every yoke of bondage that is holding Your people in captivity. We want to see Your church rise up in all of its splendor.

We want to see Your sons and daughters walk in their freedom, declaring "Who the Son of God has set free is free indeed!"

Revive us oh Lord! Not just in the church, but all through the land. Send the winds from the east, the west, the north and the south to blow on Your people, gathering them together like a great army. Let them all come singing and praising Your Holy name. Let hearts yearn for more of You. Just as the deer pants after the water brook, let our souls long after You. Let there be an earnest yearning for Your presence in our lives. Fall fresh on us Lord. Rejuvenate our souls and transform our minds in Christ Jesus so that Your thoughts will be our thoughts and Your will our will. We want a drastic change!

Revive us oh Lord! Take the very taste for alcohol and drugs out of our mouths so that we may walk soberly and upright before You. Take hatred and violence out of our hearts so that we may turn away from doing evil. Touch our hearts, oh God. Move on the hearts of whoremongers, prostitutes, fornicators, and adulterers so that they may render their bodies as a living sacrifice before You. Set us free from lying and deception, hatred and strife, gossiping and slandering, and greed and idolatry. Raise us up to be a godly people, a holy generation. Let healing, deliverance, and revival take place in our souls, in Jesus name!

God, we need a revival in the family. Cause Your sons to rise up as the priest of their homes, being faithful husbands, godly fathers, providers, protectors, leaders, and loving men of God. Then, God, cause Your daughters to be holy, chaste, and virtuous women of God. Let them be nurturers and supporters of their husbands and families. God, let husbands and wives be submitted to God and to one another, teaching their children to fear the Lord. Let Your Spirit flow through our homes. Our hearts are opened and our hands are outstretched. Father, pour out Your Spirit upon us like You did in the day of Pentecost. Let Your Spirit come like a rushing mighty wind. Revive our minds, bodies, souls and spirits in the name of Jesus!

Lord, we receive Your presence and infilling even now. We thank You for our encounter with Jesus and Holy Spirit. Our lives are forever being changed. We will never be the same. We will not forget the miracles signs and wonders that You perform in our individual lives, in our families, and in our homes. Each generation shall tell of Your goodness; and we shall forever give You all the glory, all the honor, and all the praise forever and ever. Thank You Lord for a revival! Let Your Holy Spirit take charge in the land. Thank You for refreshing and reviving Your people like only You can! We call for a worldwide revival! In Jesus' name, amen.

Minister Jacqueline Ejim
Peace and Love Ministries, Inc.
Baltimore, MD

Dear Father,

Inspirational Thought:

There is a place that we can go in the Spirit if we would dare to go after it. It is time to do a self-inventory of your spiritual walk with God and decide if you are where God would have you to be or can you go higher and deeper today. Ask the Lord to revive you so that you are lacking nothing, but totally complete in Him.

Healing for the Brokenhearted

"Give all your worries and cares to God, for He cares about you."
1 Peter 5:7

Heavenly Father, Your Word tells me You heal the brokenhearted. Dear Lord, do this for me! I am hurting and I need Your help. Heal me Lord and I shall be healed; comfort me and I shall be comforted. You are my praise!

Lord, You are the only One Who can fix my heart. I tried many things; but, they did not work. I put my faith in people and in the things of this world and was let down time after time and damaged even the more. I have been disappointed way too often. My soul is quite disturbed. Mend my broken heart dear Lord, and give me Your peace. Make me whole.

Father, I have cried so many nights for this pain to go away; but, it has been constant. It feels like my heart has been ripped into pieces and will never be put back together again. It hurts so bad that words escape me. You know God. You are fully aware of those things I feel, but find hard to articulate. It brings comfort to my heart just to know You are aware of what I have gone through and what I am going through. You know my brokenness and how I got here. You know the things that have caused me grief and pain. Nothing is hidden from You, oh Lord. You have the answers to all my pressing problems. My soul knows quite well that You are the Restorer of life. So here I am Lord with outstretched hands, and a daughter's cry saying, "Restore me Abba Father!" I release everything into Your hands. I will no longer hold onto this pain. I give it all to You. Let Your power fall upon me, the healing power of Your Spirit. I want to be made whole again. I want my joy back—that unspeakable joy that gives me strength, and no one can take away. You promised in Psalm 30:5 that, *"weeping may endure for a night, but joy cometh in the morning."* Lord, here I am waiting for the morning and the sweet joy the morning brings.

Lord, I praise You in advance for healing my brokenness. I speak victory over my life and peace to my soul. My heart is mended, and today I refuse to believe anything else except that I am healed. I am whole and free from pain. Thank You Jesus for dying on the cross, being broken in Your body so I can be healed in mine. I can be healed in my heart, in my soul, and in my mind. I will continue to keep my eyes upon You, and not those things that tried to destroy me. I will share the Good News with others! I will tell them You care about the condition of our hearts and You want us whole. Bless You Father! I praise You and thank You for making me whole. In Jesus' name I pray, amen.

Minister Ashley Hawkins-Moore
River Church of Baltimore
Baltimore, MD

My Personal Prayer for the Brokenhearted

Dear Father,

_____

_____

_____

_____

_____

_____

_____

_____

_____

_____

Inspirational Thought:

He is the Potter; you are the clay marred in His hand. Today the Potter's wheel is spinning. Feel Him putting you back together again. The pressure you feel, is His hands. And even with the pressure, He is still delicate, never intending to break you, just intending to make you, better! *"You heal the brokenhearted and bind up our wounds."* Psalm 147:3.

A Turn Around from Brokenness

"I will turn their mourning into joy. I will comfort them and exchange their sorrow for rejoicing."
Jeremiah 31:13

Dear Lord, I come before You now giving You praise, thanks, honor, and glory for You are a good and awesome God. I bless Your Holy name. You are my Father and I am Your child. I trust Your Word Lord that promises me that You would never leave nor forsake me. Your Word is true. For that, I am grateful because I need You now, more than ever.

Father, I stretch my hands to You in total submission and desperation. My heart is shattered, and my spirit is so crushed that I am barely able to speak, think, move, or breathe. The depth of pain I feel is immeasurable. I'm hurting, but yet I am numb. I am exhausted from it all. I am exhausted and exasperated, worn out and torn to pieces. It is almost too much for me to bear. I am drowning in my tears and the darkness encompasses me. I am empty but yet full with sadness and disappointment. God my soul cries out to You, oh Lamb of God! You alone are my help in times like these—when my heart is overwhelmed. The burden of my broken heart is likened to a fallen baby sparrow with broken wings. In my wounded and fragile state, You alone can save me from my suffering. Mend my broken places and put me back together again. Father, You alone are able to make me whole and give me rest from all my troubles. Your

Word says You give rest to the weary and heavy laden. As I pray these words to You in faith, I am confident that You hear my cry and trust You will answer and give rest to my weary soul.

Father, I know there is nothing I am going through that You do not already know about, as not even one sparrow can fall to the ground without You being aware of it. As my Father, You have been watching over me, waiting for this very moment—the moment when I realize I desperately need You, my heavenly Father. Step in and minister to my heart like only You can. Comfort me dear Lord. I am ready to receive all that You have for me in this moment and trust that I will emerge victoriously. I trust that in this defining moment, the healing has begun and You are rebuilding my life. Lord, thank You for making me a better version of myself. Teach me not to fret, but rather see what You are doing in the midst of it all and walk confidently in Your sovereignty and victoriously into my purpose.

I am an empty vessel before Your presence. Fill me completely, consume me entirely, so that I am overtaken by Your Spirit. Repair and resuscitate my heart. Fill me with Your Light, Your love, Your joy, Your peace, Your patience, Your grace, and Your mercy. I stand on Your promises, for You are a Promise Keeper. I come to You with hope and expectations of restoration, as I anticipate that You will touch, heal, and deliver me from my brokenness. You are the Potter, and I am the clay. Only Your skilled and mighty hands can gently and softly sift through the shattered pieces of my fragile heart and put me back together. You can take all the ugly things that I have been through and make something beautiful out of my life. Transform me God from a struggling, crawling caterpillar to a beautiful, soaring butterfly. With Your help Father, I will move freely to the next phase of my life as the person You created me to be; fearfully and wonderfully made, and completely whole.

Have Your way with me Almighty God, my Father. Mold me and shape me. Breathe Your life-giving and life-sustaining Spirit into me. Let Your Ruah course through my entire body and let it fill me to the overflow—the very breath of Your Spirit. Let Your Word flow through every broken place in my heart and revive my entire being, from the crown of my head, to the soles of my feet. As the lifter of the bowed down head, let my head be lifted with thoughts of Your goodness, faithfulness, and loving kindness. As the lover of my soul, let Your loving Spirit embrace and comfort me. Pull me from my despair and let me be reconciled to You.

As my healer, let me be healed in every aspect of my life. As my deliverer, let me be delivered from every snare of the enemy. As my helper, help me to overcome every obstacle I encounter. As a heart-fixer, let my heart be fixed to praise You in sincerity and in truth. As a mind regulator, let my mind be transformed by Your Word. As the source of my strength and the strength of my life, let Your strength be perfected in my weakness. As a miracle worker, let me see Your miracles manifest in the midst of my misery. As I surrender to You all the broken pieces of my heart, I claim restoration and declare the glory of God shall be revealed!

I rest and rock in Your arms. Thank You for giving me Your complete peace and bestowing Your healing virtues of comfort and care upon me. Thank You that my season of being brokenhearted ends today! I will see blessings in brokenness, beauty in barrenness, and benefits in betrayal. I will see my weariness turned into worthiness, my failures turned into freedom, and my woes and worries turned into wisdom to navigate through life better! And God, for all those things I did not get right the first time that I have been ashamed of, thank You that all that guilt is being replaced by Your grace and my gratitude. Let my shame and disgust bring me success. Thank You for another opportunity to see You make something beautiful out of my life. Then God, if there be any unforgiveness or thoughts of revenge in my heart, I repent and embrace Your redemption. I refuse to be broken in any area of my life! God, let my heart be pure before You.

God, I thank You that I am no longer suffering with brokenness and pain. My trials and tribulations are being turned into triumph and testimonies of Your unfailing and unfaltering goodness, grace, mercy, and love. My tears of trepidation have turned into tears of appreciation. Thank You Father for taking my tears and watering the garden of my heart until it blooms bountifully and grows strong enough that I may fulfill the purpose for which You created me.

I raise a hallelujah to You now as You have turned my mourning into dancing! I raise a hallelujah to You now as You have given me beauty for ashes! I raise a hallelujah to You now! My broken heart is healed! I honor the Spirit of the Lord Who has helped me to rise triumphantly and to be more than a conqueror. Your praise will continually be in my mouth! I will give You thanks forever! You have fixed me! It is so, and so it is, in the name of Jesus! Amen, amen, and amen!

Minister Kimberly Ponder-Thomas
The Well Christian Community Church
Livermore, CA

My Personal Prayer for a Turnaround

Dear Father,

_____

_____

_____

_____

_____

_____

_____

_____

_____

Inspirational Thought:

There is no pain that runs so deep that God cannot reach it, or has lasted for so long that God cannot heal it. Your broken heart is repairable in the Master's hand.

Bless My Family

"Behold, how good and how pleasant it is for brethren to dwell together in unity!"
Psalm 133:1

Our Father in heaven above, I come boldly to Your throne on the behalf of my family. I come to bless Your Holy name and to give You glory and honor. Thank You for all the blessings You have bestowed upon me and my family. You have been so good to us. You have loved us with an everlasting love. We love You dear God because You first loved us. You made promises to us that You have kept for You are not a man that You should lie. You promised to keep us and You have been our keeper. You promised to strengthen us when we are weak, and You have been our strength. You promised to heal us when we are sick and You have been our healer. Time after time, throughout the years, You have been faithful to my family. God, we praise You for it all! We praise You for all You have done for us and all You have been to us. We worship You! We magnify You! We lift up Your Holy name! We give You the highest praise! Hallelujah!

Father, Your Word says in Psalm 133:1, *"Behold, how good and how pleasant it is for brethren to dwell together in unity!"* This is what I pray for my family, that we dwell together in unity. I pray we will walk in agreement and be on one accord. Even in our disagreements, let our love continue for one another despite our differences. Let our love be unyielding even as Your love is for us and as You desire our love to be for one another. Let our love for each other inspire us to be accepting of one another's differences and not judgmental and contentious.

Father, You know even in families we can offend and can also be offended. I pray You teach us to forgive one another as Your Word admonishes us to do in Ephesians 4:32, *"Be kind and compassionate to one another forgiving each other, just as in Christ God forgave you."* Father help our family to remember this scripture when there is an offense—to just let it go, show compassion, and forgive. I pray we will be patient, empathetic, and kind to one another, always letting the love of God rule our hearts.

Father, when we see our family member in need, whether it is our child, parent, sibling, niece, nephew, or whomever, I pray we will not turn our backs on them. But, I pray we will help them as You provide us the grace and resources to do so. Let us be unselfish, caring, and giving. Let us bring joy into each other's lives and do each other good.

Now Lord, I pray even as You fortify us within our family unit, You will also fortify us without—protecting us from external attacks. Keep us from all hurt, harm and danger, seen and unseen, near and far. Protect my family dear Lord! Put a shield all around us. Protect us from the forces of evil and the works of the enemy. Protect us as we come and as we go. Protect us in our work and in our leisure. Keep us strong and healthy, able to do Your will. God You said our bodies are the temples of the Holy Spirit. Lord, I pray we yield our bodies to You and cultivate a personal relationship with You. Be our God dear Lord and make us Your people. Let none perish in our family, Lord. But, let them all come to the salvation knowledge of Jesus.

Dear Father, let us come together and worship You as a family. Let us remember Your goodness and Your grace. Let us walk in paths of righteousness doing what is acceptable and pleasing in Your sight. Let our hearts be knitted together with our Savior. Keep us together and keep us covered under Your precious blood. Let Your Holy Spirit be our Guide and lead our family into a meaningful and fruitful relationship with You.

Father, thank You over and over again. You have indeed been good to us. Let us remember Your goodness and Your grace and bless Your Holy name. We worship and adore You, in Jesus' name, amen.

Evangelist Mary A. Fitzgerald
Christian Life Church
Baltimore, MD

My Personal Prayer for My Family

Dear Father,

_____

_____

_____

_____

_____

_____

_____

_____

Inspirational Thought:

The family is a large and complicated body of members, each member with his or her own identity, thoughts, beliefs, and lifestyles. And, many times those variables can clash within the family, bringing a rift. But do not fret over any breaks within Your family, no matter how large or small. God is a healer, a mender, and a fixer. He can put Your family back together again. Do not give up. Keep praying and calling their names out before the Lord and watch what the Lord will do.

Cover My Family Dear Lord

"We love because He first loved us."
1 John 4:19

In the precious name of Jesus, I come to You Father to say, "Thank You!" Thank You for blessing and keeping me. Thank You for giving me a heart and mind to intercede for my family. Thank You for this posture of prayer. I lift up this prayer asking that it be a sweet savor in Your nostrils and a soothing sound to Your ears. Father, God, I prayer cover my family in the name of Jesus. Your Word says if I ask anything in Your Son Jesus' name, You will answer.

Father, I come before Your throne on the behalf of my family. I ask dear Lord that You be with each one of my family members. Let none of the schemes and tactics of the enemy prevail against them. I pray You cover them with Your feathers and hide them under Your wings. Dispatch Your angels around them to protect and defend them from seen and unseen dangers. *"For we wrestle not against flesh and blood, but against principalities, against powers, against the rulers of the darkness of this world, against spiritual wickedness in high places."* (Ephesians 6:12).

Lord, I decree and declare that my family is victorious and no weapon formed against us will prosper because You go before us. We are healed by Your stripes and covered by Your blood. We are the head and not the tail. We are strong in You, Lord and in the power of Your might. I decree and declare we will not see premature deaths in our family, but with long life will You satisfy us and show us Your salvation. You are our protector. You are everything that we need. You are the great I am in our lives and we give You glory.

Father, my heart's cry is not just for my family's physical safety, but I am also praying for our spiritual wellbeing. Let us live out our God given purpose and let nothing prevent Your plans from coming to fruition in our lives. I decree and declare, Your kingdom come and Your will be done on earth as it is in heaven concerning our lives. I decree and declare, Your plans and Your purpose be manifested in our lives to the glory of God. Father, I am confident that You have a plan for each one of us from the youngest to the eldest and the least to the greatest. Jeremiah 29:11 says, *"For, I know the plans that I have for you declares the Lord, plans to prosper you; not to harm you. Plans to give you a hope and a future."* Your Word is our promise. It is our hope!

Father, even as I pray these prayers of blessings over my family, I want to thank You for what You have already done for us and what You are still doing in our lives. You have been our provider, protector and deliverer. You have been our comforter and keeper. You have been keeping us close—molding and shaping us, for You are the Potter and we are the clay. Continue to have Your way dear God. Let everyone of my family members recognize that You have always been a presence in our lives and a faithful friend. Let us see You as the Author and Finisher of our faith. Let us know You as Alpha and Omega, our beginning, our ending, and everything in between. Most importantly, let us know You as our Redeemer, our Savior, our soon coming King. Let my family render our lives unto You, completely. Let them recognize Your goodness and give You all the praise, glory, and honor for being so loving and compassionate toward us. Let us sing Your praises!

Now God, I pray for the elders of our family. Bless them as they come and as they go. Bless them in their golden years just as You blessed Sarah and Abraham, and Zachariah and Elizabeth. Be with them as they go about their day and strengthen their bodies and minds. Cause them to flourish and be fruitful even in their old age.

God, I pray for the men of our family. Keep our men on Your mind, protecting them from the wiles and attacks of the enemy. Give them the strength and courage to stand against the enemy when their faith is being challenged, and when they are being enticed by the desires of this world. Let them stay connected to You and be steadfast, unmovable, always abounding in the work of the Lord. Give them dreams and visions as You did with Moses, Solomon, Joseph, Daniel, and the men of old. Speak to them and let the power of the Holy Spirit guide their footsteps. Let them be the men of God You called them to be—leaders, teachers, and protectors of their families. Make them to be mighty men of valor, always standing for righteousness and truth.

God, I pray for the women of our family. Father, help us to be virtuous women understanding our purpose, value, and worth. Help us to be focused on the call of God that is on our lives and to stand firm in that call. Help us not to shy away from our calling to be nurturers to our children and family. Give us discernment and wisdom as You gave to Esther, Deborah, Naomi, and other mighty women of God. Let us operate in that motherly instinct You deposited in us, so that we can walk in discernment and wisdom as we prayer cover our family.

Father, when the women of my family get discouraged and heavy laden, let us be confident in knowing that we are special in Your sight and the apple of Your eyes. Open our eyes to see we are blessed far beyond our circumstances, and we are more than conquerors in Christ Jesus. We are Your gift to our family and a precious diadem in Your hands. Let us recognize our value!

God, I pray for the children of our family. Father put a hedge of protection around them. Send angels to protect their eye gates and ear gates. Preserve their innocence in this perverse world. I pray they be trained up in the Word of God so that when they are old, they will not depart from it. Lord, let our children not be confused about their identity or purpose. Help them to walk in self-assurance of who they are in You, and what You have called them to do. Let them move about in the realm of the earth with divine purpose so that they will make a kingdom impact for Your glory, honor, and praise.

Now Father, as I closed this prayer, I am thankful that my family is more than blessed. I declare, You have prepared a table before us in the presence of our enemies. You have anointed our heads with oil, and our cups run over. You have opened the windows of heaven and poured us out blessings. All that we have ever needed, Your hands have provided. You will do us good all the days of our lives. I give You all the praise on the behalf of my family. It is in Jesus' mighty name that I offer this prayer. Amen, amen and amen.

Minister Monica Levine Brunson
Anointed House of Prayer Ministries
Baltimore, MD

My Personal Prayer for a Covering over My Family

Dear Father,

_____

_____

_____

_____

_____

_____

_____

_____

_____

_____

_____

_____

Inspirational Thought:

"As for me and my house, we will serve the Lord." Joshua 24:15.

A Prayer for Our Sons and Daughters

"And I will be your Father, and you will be My sons and daughters,
says the LORD Almighty."
2 Corinthians 6:18

O Most Holy and Righteous God, how excellent and majestic is Your name in all the earth. There is no one greater than You. You have no rival. You have no equal. You are God alone! You reign forever and Your kingdom shall have no end. We bow before You in humble submission, casting all our crowns at Your feet. We worship You. We praise You. We bless Your Holy name! Now Spirit of the Living God, fall fresh on us as we come boldly before Your throne of grace to lift up our sons and our daughters unto You. You said if we ask anything in Your name, it will be done. So, let it be done unto us according to our faith.

Dear Father, we ask for our sons to be delivered from a spirit of complacency, fear, and uncertainty! Release confidence and power over their lives. Draw them into destiny. Let them seek You as it concerns Your will and their purpose. Reveal to them, Lord, Your plans for their lives because You have a hope and a future, an expected end for them. Bind every snare, scheme, plot, and plan of the enemy that seeks to keep them from knowing You and knowing their God given assignment.

Father, we pray for our sons' appetites. Let them hunger and thirst after You, the living God, so their lives will be richly blessed. Lord, let Your Word reach them and let them receive it—hiding it in their hearts and applying it to their lives. Loose the bands of the enemy and raise our sons up to be the men of God You created them to be. Help them to be warriors of the Word, a prophetic voice in their generation, and powerful vessels of honor for Your will and good pleasure! Let them have great expectations. Let them expect promotions, elevation, and favor. Give them opportunities that they have not had before and open new doors unto them. Provide them with gainful employment and let them see they are prosperous in You.

Father, if our sons are seeking a wife, let them obtain favor from You, and find their good thing for You said in Your Word, *"He who finds a wife finds a good thing, And obtains favor from the Lord."* (Proverbs 18:22). Father, pour out Your favor upon our sons and let them seek to be connected to the wife You have uniquely designed for them. And then Lord, when their aspirations seem to be stalled, God let peace rule their hearts and minds. Help them to be level headed. Remove frustration, aggravation, and agitation that may try to rise up in them; and help them to be patient and to wait on You. God, You know what they stand in need of and we trust You will provide it. We thank You in advance for all these things and give You praise!

Now Father, we apply the blood of Jesus over our sons! Bless their going out and their coming in, their work and their leisure, their laying down and their rising up! Draw them with Your love so they in turn will know how to love. Arise, oh God and take Your place in their hearts. Let them acknowledge You as their Redeemer, their Lord, and their soon coming King! Holy Spirit, help them to rise up and take their rightful place in the body of Christ. Let them be ministers of the Gospel and witnesses in the earth. Holy Spirit, anoint them afresh! Meet every need and fill every void. Let there be nothing missing, nothing lacking, and nothing broken in their lives. God, let them be a light in this world, and salt in the earth so others will come to know You, and give You glory.

Dear Father, let bountiful blessings chase them down and overtake them. Give our sons the confidence to pursue everything You have for them. Lord, help them to be discerning of those who cannot go on this journey with them. Give them wisdom concerning their choice of friends and associates. Remove people, places, or practices that seek to keep them from walking in their purpose. Destroy yokes, lift burdens, and break bondages and strongholds that would try to hinder our sons. We decree that our sons shall be men of valor, confident, righteous, and prosperous in all their ways. Align their will with Your will. Let their decree be "There is a king in me!" You get the glory, oh God!

O God, now we lift up our daughters before You. We decree that our daughters are precious in Your sight and You have a plan for their lives. Lord, we ask that You would speak to their hearts and direct their paths. Order their steps in Your Word! Let them rise up and be who You called them to be, realizing there are great possibilities before them, and they are not limited by their gender. Help our daughters to know they are destined for greatness. We pray they excel academically, financially, emotionally, spiritually, socially, and physically. Help them to stay focused and on task. Remove anything that would distract them from their goals and deter them from their future! We come against any spirit that seeks to keep our daughters bound, stagnated, depressed, and full of anxiety. We decree and declare it will not prosper and that our daughters will shine and excel in all of their endeavors, in Jesus name. I pray our daughters will have a determination to go all the way in their academics, their ministry, their businesses, and in all they put their hands to do—breaking glass ceilings! Let them be confident, knowing their own worth so that they will not be jealous or envious of their fellow sister; but willing to support her. Let them be kind enough to work alongside their sister in unity and harmony.

Father, bless our daughters throughout this day. Safeguard them, for they are precious in Your sight. Protect them physically, mentally and socially. Lead and guide them into manifold blessings, and let them be a blessing to others. Let them be that Proverbs 31 woman who not only took care of herself, but also her entire household and community.

Now Lord, we pray You will give our daughters favor. Those daughters, who desire to marry, let their kings find them. Raise up priests, providers, and protectors for our daughters. Raise up men that will do them good and not evil. For those who are already married, we thank You God that their husbands will know their worth and treat them as daughters of the Most High God, showering them with Your love.

God, let Your daughters walk in Your favor, knowing that they are blessed and highly favored. Let them not worry: worry about their children, worry about their husbands, worry about their marriages, worry about their families, or worry about their health. But God, grant our daughters Your peace, love, and joy. Let them feel You ever so close, especially in those times when they feel alone and uncertain about life.

Father, we pray a special prayer over our daughters' bodies. In the name of Jesus, touch every area, now! Where there is pain, release Your healing. Where there is sickness and disease, we declare by Your stripes they are healed. Where there are maladies and improper body functions, we pray that order arise, and every part of their bodies will hear Your voice and come into proper alignment. We pray over their reproductive systems. For our daughters who desire to be mothers, we come against infertility, barrenness, miscarriages, birth defects, premature births, and even death during childbirth! We speak healthy pregnancies, healthy babies, and easy deliveries!

Oh God, be with our daughters. Guide them. Lead them. Comfort them. Protect them and bless them indeed. Let Your Word be a lamp unto their feet and a light unto their path. Make Your countenance to shine upon them. When they are weak, be their strength. When they are discouraged, be the lifter of their heads. When they are unsure, be the compass for their way. When they are afraid, let them know they have no reason to fear. When they are feeling rejected, unwanted, and unaccepted, be their friend. And, when they are sad, restore the joy of their salvation.

Thank You for the prayers You have helped us to pray over our sons and daughters. We pray they will walk in Your statues all the days of their lives, obey Your voice, and be blessed! In Jesus' mighty, majestic, marvelous, and miraculous name we pray. Amen!

Pastor Anita P. Latin, M.Th.
Visionary of Abounding Love Bible Ministry
Rodeo, CA

My Personal Prayer for Our Sons and Daughters

Dear Father,

_____

_____

_____

_____

_____

_____

_____

_____

_____

_____

Inspirational Thought:

Your son... your daughter is dear to you. Yes indeed! But, they are also dear to God! Trust that He loves them and wants the best for them. Their lives are in His hand, and He will take care of them all the days of their lives.

A Prayer for Our Children

"Lo, children are an heritage of the LORD: and the fruit of the womb is His reward."
Psalm 127:3

Dear Father God, I thank You for waking me up this morning with a heart and mind to praise You. I bless You Father because You are so good to Your children. You meet all of our needs according to Your riches in glory. I thank You Lord that You hear us when we pray and call on Your name. Your Word tells us in John 17:7, if we abide in You and Your Word in us, we can ask whatsoever we will, and it will be done unto us. So, God, I pray You will answer the prayers that are lifted up unto You today on the behalf of our sons and our daughters.

God these are perilous times and we need You now, more than ever. Psalm 127:3 says, *"Lo, Children are a heritage of the Lord and the fruit of the womb is His reward."* Our sons and daughters are gifts from You Lord. We thank You for them, and we are asking that You will protect and keep them wherever they may go. In their homes, in their school houses, in public arenas, and in their travels, protect and shield them from all evil, hurt, harm, and danger. Safeguard them from any satanic force that would try to come up against them. Father, anything that would try to diminish them or even destroy them, we pray You will disrupt it and not allow it to prosper in their lives. We thank You for Your protection over them. Let their homes be their sanctuary and let their schools be a great place for learning, growing and creating some of their best experiences. Open the eyes of their understanding to what is being taught. Give them the Spirit of the Learned.

Father, even for our older children who are faced with college decisions, open up doors of opportunities, provide scholarships, and financial assistance. Remove any financial barriers that would keep them from gaining a higher education. For our children who live on college campuses, please keep them safe. Shield and protect them. Set a watch over everything that concerns them. Anoint their minds and keep them away from activities that would cause them harm. Help them to make wise decisions. When they are faced with right or wrong, let them always choose to do right. When they are faced with choosing the world or choosing You, let their hearts be drawn to You. I pray they will be leaders and not followers, and if followers, they will follow only after that which is good. Let them be the head and not the tail, above only and never beneath. Let them rise up to be lenders and not borrowers. Let them find favor with God and with man, all for Your glory.

God, we pray concerning our children's selection of friends and associates. Help them to choose friends and associates that will do them good and not evil. And then God, remove those around them who are a bad influence in their lives. Remove those who try to persuade them to go down wayward paths and steer them away from their God given purpose. Surround them with peers who will be a positive influence and a godsend.

Father above all else, we ask that You would give our children a heart after You. Let their desire be for the things of God. Even with all the various activities, attractions, and distractions in the world, let them still yearn to be in the house of the Lord in Your presence. Give youth pastors, leaders, and workers the wisdom needed to plan activities that will actively engage our children, capture their attention, and draw them closer to You. Father, I pray that our children will not be attracted and enticed by the things of this world. I bind every effort of the devil to steal their souls!

Father, anoint parents and guardians to be sensitive enough to hear Your voice regarding what their child may be dealing with and what they may need. Help us to understand what they need to grow into mature men and women of God. Help our prayers to be specific and tailored-made for each child to address their assignment and purpose in life. God, even now, You know what our children are facing. You know their inner struggles. Touch those who are being belittled and bullied and being made to feel less than who they really are. Touch those who are dealing with self hatred, a lack of confidence, and low self-esteem. Touch those who are confused about their identity and sexuality. Father, we know confusion is not of You. Satan would love to keep our children in a state of confusion. But, I bind up confusion in the name of Jesus! Lord, I pray, You clear their minds and help them to know who they are and what You have called them to do.

Dear God, for our children who have gone astray I call them back to You, back into the Kingdom, and back into the household of faith. God Your Word promises us in Proverbs 22:6 to *"Train up a child in the way he should go: and when he is old, he will not depart from it."* So, God, please bring our children back—those who have strayed away. God, draw them by Your Spirit, and let us not stop praying and believing for their deliverance and their salvation. Let them know that no matter where they are, they can always call on

You and find help in the time of trouble. Thank You Lord that Your hands are upon them and they are protected by You.

Now Lord, I pray You touch every reader and intercessor of this book—everyone who will pray these prayers and believe by faith that You hear them. Let the prayers be a blessing to them, and make a difference in the lives of their love ones who they are praying for on today. Let the sisters praying these prayers see a change in their children and in their family members. Let them be strengthened and encouraged as they pray these prayers of faith, trusting and believing that You know exactly what Your people need, and You know how to bless them.

Thank You for the opportunity to pray for Your people. I pray You honor this prayer in the name of Your son Jesus Christ. Amen and amen.

Dr. Denise L. Madden
Christian Life Church
Baltimore, MD

My Personal Prayer for Our Children

Dear Father,

_____

_____

_____

_____

_____

_____

_____

_____

_____

Inspirational Thought:

Don't give up on your child. God has not and He will not give up on you.

Prayer against the Exploitation of Our Children

"Thus saith the Lord; A voice was heard in Ramah, lamentation, and bitter weeping; Rahel weeping for her children refused to be comforted for her children, because they were not."
Jeremiah 31:15

Dear Lord, You are the giver of life. You made us and not we ourselves. We thank You for life and we thank You for the lives of our children. We come before You to intercede for our children who are losing their lives every day and are being exploited. Hear our cries for the children of our nation. Forgive us for allowing so many of them to perish on our watch.

Dear God, forgive us for taking our children lives even before they are birthed from their mother's womb. Father, we know there are many reasons why women and their families may decide not to have their child, but God we are asking that they will acknowledge You in all their ways and You will direct their paths. We pray, you will lead and guide them to do what is right in Your sight, so our children will live and not die. God help us to seek to please You in all our ways. Then Father, we know there are many families who desire to have children, but physically are unable. We pray You will make divine connections, and touch hearts and minds so there will be less abortions and more adoptions. We pray for a divine hook up between those with unwanted pregnancies and those who are barren but want to provide a loving home for a child. Lord, we are praying for a remedy—a solution to this abortion epidemic. Lord, stop the massive bleed—the bleeding that takes place in the abortion clinics and the bleeding that takes place on our streets with our children being gunned down. Lord, protect our children in the womb, on the streets, in their schools, and even in their own homes. Let them not be plucked up in the days of their youth. Keep them from premature death—whether in the womb or outside of the womb. Let them live and not die and declare the works of the Lord in their generation. Keep them from being a victim of crime or even an assailant. Let them grow up and rise up to be a blessing to their nation. Let them live a full, healthy, godly life. God help our children! Stop the bleeding! Stop the killings!

Lord, we pray for the many children who go missing around the world. We pray for those children who are being kidnapped, taken into human trafficking, sold into slavery, sacrificed, and those who end up in the hands of those who unmercifully torment them day and night. Lord, we pray for Your angels to rescue them. Lord, open prison doors so these young captives can be set free. Deliver God as only You can. Mothers, fathers, and families are waiting for their child to return home safe and sound. Let an urgency come upon the body of Christ to intercede for our children who are dying, exploited, and held in captivity. Let churches rise up and make this a part of their kingdom agenda to pray like never before for our children. Let our faith based institutions bring awareness to this devastation in our nation. Let there be prayer visuals and prayer watches organized daily around the clock on behalf of our missing sons and daughters.

Then Lord, we pray for our children who are being drawn away by their own lust. We pray for children who are motherless and/or fatherless, seeking love and acceptance in all the wrong places. We pray for You to protect them in their vulnerability. Keep them in their right state of mind and not so easily enticed, lured into danger. Keep them from connecting and making alliances with dangerous people. Keep them from making bad decisions to indulge in drugs, mind altering substances, and reckless living. Keep them from out of the streets dear God. Give them a safe haven, a safe place to be loved and taught right from wrong. Let our young people grow into the person You would have them to be.

Lord, there is nothing hidden that will not be revealed, nothing done in the dark that will not be exposed in the light, and nothing whispered in secret rooms that will not be proclaimed on the housetops. Lord, let the truth be released concerning everything that is happening to the children around the world. Let a burden be released on the body of Christ to join together as one to protect the youth of our nation and to bring them back home. In Jesus' name, we pray, amen.

Minister Karen Brown,
Campaign for Souls
Middletown, DE

My Personal Prayer against the Exploitation of Our Children

Dear Father,

_____

_____

_____

_____

_____

_____

_____

_____

_____

_____

_____

Inspirational Thought:

"Children are a gift from God. They are a reward from Him."
Psalm 127:3

God Over Marriages

"Be completely humble and gentle; be patient, bearing with one another in love. Make every effort to keep the unity of the Spirit through the bond of peace."
Ephesians 4:2-3

Dear awesome and wonderful God, You said in Jeremiah 33:3 to call upon You and You would show us great and mighty things that we know not. God, we are calling upon You and declaring Your name over our marriages. Hear us when we call, in Jesus name.

Dear El Elyon, "Lord Most High," we lift the sanctity of marriages up to You today. When our marriages are in turmoil be Jehovah-Shalom, "The Lord Our Peace". Let Your peace overtake our households so that all who enter in will know that You are there. Father, when we lack the necessities of life, be our Jehovah-Jireh, "The Lord Our Provider." Provide us with what we need in our homes and in our marriages. Help us to be good stewards, grateful, and on one accord—agreeing on how to utilize what You have generously given unto us.

Father, thank You for the gift of each other. Make us whole and keep us well so that we can be at our best for one another. If there are any physical and/or emotional infirmities in our bodies be our Jehovah-Rapha, "The Lord Who Heals." Help us to walk in divine health, able to enjoy the marriages You have given us. Heal any and every sickness and disease. Break generational curses and cause demonic attacks against our marriages and families to flee. God, let the words we speak to our spouse never inflict pain or damage to them. But rather, let our words be healing to their soul. And, if at any time our words have offended our spouse and have caused them pain, we pray Your forgiveness and ask that You touch their heart and heal every broken place. When our communication fails, let Your Word be our help and our measuring stick. Let Your Word guide our words so that we speak to one another with grace and understanding. Guide our words and our actions so that they will be pleasing to You. You are able to sanctify us holy, for You are Jehovah-M'Kaddesh, "The Lord Who Sanctifies and Makes Holy." Lord, sanctify us. Make us holy before You and one another. Even when temptation tries to seep its way into our marriages to draw us in ungodly directions to entertain ungodly matters, remind us that we are not enslaved to our flesh but are guided by Your Word and Your Holy Spirit. Remove and break all ungodly soul-ties. Remind us that You are our Jehovah-Tsidkenu, "The Lord Our Righteousness" and in You we can make right decisions for our union.

Then Father, on days that we look for our spouse to be our everything and our desire goes unfulfilled, help us to recognize that our spouse is not our God, and we should never put that kind of expectation on them. They cannot be our all and all, always available to meet our needs. Help us to be satisfied in knowing "The Lord Is There," our Jehovah-Shammah. You will satisfy us and meet our needs. Help us to wrap our expectations up in You. You are our all and all—our comfort, our peace, and our joy for each new day. You alone are our everything and will always be there. You are our El-Olam "Everlasting God." Let us find strength in knowing that

You will be an everlasting presence in our marriages. As the Everlasting God in our marriages, when things get tough, we can look to You to be our help. On our best days, make our marriages even better, and on our worst days bring back to our remembrance our best days. Be forever present, the Everlasting God in our union. When the enemy surrounds us, remind us to call on Jehovah Sabaoth, "The Lord of Hosts" Who will deliver. You are indeed the help of our marriages. You are the Everlasting God, The Lord of Hosts!

You are Elohim, the "The Supreme and Mighty One," Creator of all things. God, we pray for creativity in our marriages. Give us the mindset to create new and wonderful memories every day. We speak favor over our marriage and that the favor of God will follow us everywhere we go. We speak wholeness and holiness over our marriage and declare that love will abide in every aspect. Let our intimacy with each other and with You be a never-ending joy. In Jesus' name. Amen.

Elder Shelley Spence
Messiah CC Church
Reisterstown, MD

My Personal Prayer for God Over Marriages

Dear Father,

_____

_____

_____

_____

_____

_____

_____

_____

_____

_____

_____

Inspirational Thought:

Let your marriage be a three-strand cord—you, your spouse, and the Almighty God. A three-strand cord is not easily broken. God wants to be involved.

A Prayer for Marriages

"For husbands, this means love your wives, just as Christ loved the church. He gave up His life for her." Ephesians 5:25

Abba, from the beginning of time You ordained marriage. You have shown us in Your Word that Your desire for marriage is that it should reflect the love Christ has for His church. Father, many have entered into the marriage covenant; but, many are struggling to keep it. I pray for those who are in the early stages of marriage, where perhaps they are beginning to realize things are not working out as they had planned, and feelings of disillusionment have replaced trust and enthusiasm. Father, I pray You would increase their patience in the face of unmet expectations and help them to exercise long-suffering in the face of troubling circumstances as differences are being worked out and prayed through.

God, I pray for those who may be dealing with seasons of misunderstandings in their marriage. Help them Father! Right now, they may be struggling to hold on to their joy and to their peace because interpersonal relationships can be really challenging! But despite the challenges, Your Word says that trust must be placed in You. You are able to pull them through the hurdles and turbulent times if they would hold on to their faith. Help them to trust You while working through life's challenges and marital matters. Most of all, Father drive out the spirit of offense. This is where oftentimes the enemy has Your people stuck. But You have given them the power over all the works of the enemy. Help them to continually pray against the spirit of offense so that no bitter root will enter into their marriage. It must not be allowed! Father God, help them to practice forgiveness and to keep Jesus in the middle of it all.

Father, remind husbands and wives that You are the God of restoration. You promised to restore what has been stolen and that includes marriages. There is hope! Restore those marriages that are crumbling and bring them back into alignment with Your perfect will according to Your good Word. Father, drive out the works of the enemy. Drive out his lies and his schemes and teach Your people how to travail for their marriages and not be tempted to give up and give in so easily. Teach them how to collaborate with You, to listen to Your voice, and follow Your lead in their marriage because marriage is Your idea and divine order. Help them to look to You first and foremost and then seek the wise counsel of men.

Now, Father for those marriages that are still maturing, yet stable and committed, I pray that they will share their victories and challenges with those who may need help. I pray those marriages will help struggling marriages to grow and become conformed to the pattern of how Christ is with His church—committed and loving her unconditionally, every day. Lord, I continue to trust that as You are patient and loving with the church, we will be the same in our marriages. Lord, I pray You will give our marriages beauty for ashes, joy for mourning and a garment of praise for the spirit of heaviness. Dear Lord, cover our marriages in difficult times. We thank You for Your covering and Your consistency. We thank You for Your faithfulness and Your plans You have for our marriages. Your plans are good. They are not designed to harm us. So, we can rest securely in the plans You have laid out for our marriages and for our future.

Now, Father we pray, let those who have entered into the marriage covenant become one, not only in flesh, but in heart and mind. Help them to consistently operate in the fruits of the Spirit—love, joy, peace, long-suffering, gentleness, goodness, faith, meekness, and self-control. Let our marriages bring You glory, honor and praise! God, we trust You to do it. We believe You have a plan no matter what it looks like and we declare marriages are a gift from God.

Now, unto Him Who can do so much more than we can ask or even think, to the only wise God, Whose faithfulness remains constant and Whose mercies are new every morning, I offer this prayer on behalf of marriages everywhere, at every age and every stage. Amen.

Lady Fay S. Bair
Christian Life Church
Baltimore, MD

My Personal Prayer for Marriages

Dear Father,

_____

_____

_____

_____

_____

_____

_____

_____

_____

_____

Inspirational Thought:

God loves marriage. It is God's example of His relationship with the church. Do not give up on your marriage. God has not given up on you.

A Prayer for the Lonely and Forgotten

"It is the Lord who goes before you. He will be with you; He will not leave you or forsake you. Do not fear or be dismayed."
Deuteronomy 31:8

Glory to Your name Father, God! How I worship You! How I praise Your glorious name! You are a good, good Father, and I know I am loved by You.

God, when I am all alone feeling lonely and forgotten, I draw strength from You. Despite who has walked away from me, forsaken or betrayed me, I take comfort in knowing You have an immeasurable and unyielding love for me and will never abandon me. I take courage in knowing You see me and see the condition of my heart because You are El Roi, "The God Who sees me". You know when I am feeling lonely, and because of Your great compassion, You have been my help. When loneliness tried to bring an assault against my relationship with You and make me feel like I had been abandoned by You, thank You for helping me to stand on Your truth—You will never leave nor forsake me.

Lord, I thank You that You are not only with me, but You are Yahweh Shamar, "The God Who keeps me". It has been in my greatest times of loneliness that You have kept me. You kept my heart from fainting and my mind at ease.   Just to know You were there was enough. Thank You for covering my mind and covering my emotions.

Father, thank You for helping me to embrace where I am in this stage of my life. Although, I may be the only one in the room, or the only one at the dinner table, or the only one where I lay my head at night, I realize I am not alone. But, I am with You and You are with me. I dwell in the secret place, under Your shadow, oh Most High God. I resist the urge to feel lonely or forgotten when You are here with me. You are my stability and security. You uphold me and You will never leave or forsake me.

When loneliness tried to creep in, I longed and thirsted after You. In that solitary place, where my soul was afflicted with emotions I could not fully process, I longed and thirsted after You. To my delight, You satisfied me with Your presence and quenched the longing of my soul. Lord, I welcome being in Your presence because in Your presence is the fullness of joy and at Your right hand are pleasures forever more. I have that joy! Thank You God! Thank You Lord— when I felt lonely, when I felt forsaken, and when I felt like I had been forgotten, You brought me into Your presence and filled me with Your peace and unspeakable joy. You settled me and quieted my soul.

Father, I thank You for helping me to see that You are always there. You will never abandon me. You will never forsake me. You will never forget me. I have consolation in knowing that I am inscribed in the palms of Your hands. It gives me peace. I do not have to feel lonely or forgotten, no matter what is going on in my life. Tribulations cannot separate us. Distresses cannot separate us. Things present or things to come cannot separate us. Nothing in all creation can separate me from Your love—the love of Jesus, my

Lord. You surround me with Your love, joy and peace—peace that surpasses my understanding and keeps my heart from being troubled.

So, Lord, in those days when loneliness attempts to rise up against me, creating a false narrative in my life that I have been forgotten, let me not only remember that You could never forget me, but also that You have a plan for my life. Therefore God, I wait on You. You are my constant guide and companion. Thank You, Holy Spirit, for speaking to my soul—saying, "Hope in God." Thank You for putting a new song in my heart, a song of praise unto You. You are a shield for me, my glory, and the lifter of my head. I am never alone and I will not be forgotten. I will trust in Your steadfast love and rejoice in Your salvation. I take delight in Your presence. You are with me and will never leave me. For this, I give You praise, in Jesus' name. Amen.

Minister Alicia M. Finley
Landmark Restoration Christian Fellowship
Oakland, CA

My Personal Prayer for the Lonely and the Forgotten

Dear Father,

_____

_____

_____

_____

_____

_____

_____

_____

Inspirational Thought:

When You are feeling lonely and forgotten, remember the Word of God that says, *"You hem me in behind and before, and You lay Your hand upon me. Such knowledge is too wonderful for me, too lofty for me to attain. Where can I go from Your Spirit? Where can I flee from Your presence? If I go up to the heavens, You are there; if I make my bed in the depths, You are there. If I rise on the wings of the dawn, if I settle on the far side of the sea, even there Your hand will guide me, Your right hand will hold me fast."*
Psalm 139:5-10.

Comfort for those Who Mourn

"Blessed are they that mourn: for they shall be comforted."
Matthew 5:4

Father God in the name of Jesus, I lift You up. I exalt You and I magnify Your Holy name. You are great in all of Your ways, from everlasting to everlasting. We thank You for loving us and caring about what we go through. We thank You that in our times of distress, You will never leave nor forsake us. We are never alone; no not ever alone because You are always by our side. Lord, we want to feel You in our times of distress, in our times of sadness, and in our times of sorrow.

Father, I am confident that You are acquainted with our grief and our sorrow. You see our brokenness. You know about our losses and how painful that is to our hearts. Please Lord, mend our broken hearts in the name of Jesus. We have lost those so dear to us— mothers, fathers, sons, daughters, siblings, spouses and friends. Lives have been lost through accidents, sicknesses and diseases, murders on the streets, traumatic occurrences, and other unfortunate circumstances. So many lives have been lost and therefore, so many hearts are heavy, hurting and grieving. Oh God, we mourn with those who mourn. We weep with those who weep. God be our help. Many times God, we did not know how to handle our grief and we did not think we would make it through it. But

God, when the grief got too heavy for us to bear, You stepped right in and was a present help. You are our burden bearer and our way maker. I just want to say, thank You.

God for the ones who are still buried in grief with their heads hung down low in sorrow and sadness, let Your Word be the lifter of their heads. Let them proclaim, *"I will lift up my eyes unto the hill from whence cometh my help. My help cometh from the Lord, Who made heaven and earth."* (Psalm 121:1-2). Let Your Word, through the Holy Spirit, minister Your peace, joy, and goodness to their hearts. Jesus, our Lord, intercede for them. Intercede for us. We all need You.

God, thank You that Your Word covers us. Your Word gives us the hope that we need in our time of mourning. We thank You for letting us know that our grief and pain will not last always for Your Word tells us, *"...weeping may endure for the night, but joy shall come in the morning."* (Psalm 30:5). God, we might not know how long our night will last before the morning comes. But glory to God, we know the morning will come. We know it will not last always. You will dry our tears. You will arrest our pain. You will comfort our hearts. You will bring back our joy. And in the meantime, on this night's journey, we know we are still growing and learning life's lessons that will help us somehow and someway. So, thank You Lord!

Now, we pray You will release Your angels around those families that are still mourning. Let Your angels minister strength and peace to their weary souls, for You said, *"Blessed are they that mourn for they shall be comforted."* (Matthew 5:4). Thank You for comforting those who mourn—those who are brokenhearted.

Lord, we rejoice even at this time for the years You have given us with our love ones, and we pray that we hold onto the sweet joyful memories of them. We pray that we will also remember that because of the everlasting life we have through Jesus Christ, we will see our love ones again seated around the throne. God, we thank You for keeping us until then and making life joyful once again. We thank You for the blessings of each new day! We anticipate great things are going to happen in our lives despite what we have been through. We believe to see the goodness of the Lord in the land of the living. Thank You, God. Thank You for Your peace and joy. Thank You for settling our hearts so that we can now say, "All is well." God, we give You praise in Jesus' name. Amen.

Reverend Connie E. Wood
Greater New Hope Baptist Church
Baltimore, MD

My Personal Prayer of Comfort for Those Who Mourn

Dear Father,

_____

_____

_____

_____

_____

_____

_____

_____

_____

_____

Inspirational Thought:

"Lift up your heads, O ye gates; and be ye lift up, ye everlasting doors; and the King of glory shall come in. Who is this King of glory? The LORD strong and mighty, the LORD mighty in battle. Lift up your heads, O ye gates; even lift them up, ye everlasting doors; and the King of glory shall come in. Who is this King of glory? The LORD of hosts, He is the King of glory." Psalms 24:7-10

Where are You Lord?

"And the God of all grace, Who called you to His eternal glory in Christ, after you have suffered a little while, will Himself restore you and make you strong, firm and steadfast. To Him be the power forever and ever. Amen"

I Peter 5:10, 11

"Daughter, your faith has made you well. Go in peace. Your suffering is over."

Mark 5:34

Abba Father, this is a place where I can barely utter a word. My thoughts keep casting shadows. This is a darkness I could never have imagined. Where are You? My heart is shattered beyond all hope of recovering. I do not know how to do this. I do not know how to move in or pass this place of impossible pain. I have lost loved ones before. But this one—Lord, this one feels unbearable. I asked You not to allow the breath to leave his body. I begged You but You let him die. I am angry. I am filled with a pain that threatens to take my breath away once and for all. It feels like that would be a welcome escape from this broken heart, this shattered soul.

I am angry. Yet, I am afraid to direct my anger towards You. Who have I in heaven but You? Where else can I go? Where else can I even hope to find help, hope, and healing? In the depths of my grief, I do not feel like I want to be helped. I only want to be gone from this time—this place. You have disappointed me Father. The disappointment has taken me to a place of faithlessness. Where were You? Where are You now? I do not feel You. I do not see You. I am too disillusioned to even hope for hope. I want to be gone from the travesty of this darkness. My mind is in a fog. I cannot seem to put one thought in front of the other. I feel so weak, so vulnerable, and so hopeless.

The only resounding thoughts are the "Whys" and the "What ifs". You could have kept him from dying. But You did not. Why? What if I had done something different? What if I had known it would be the last time I would see him alive, on this side of heaven? It torments me to know those were our final moments together here on earth when I sat across the table from him that last day, that last time, sharing that last meal. I had not an inkling of what was to come in a few short hours. He would be gone and it would feel like You were gone as well.

Father, I fell headlong into a crisis of faith. This was the most crucial thing I have asked of You and still, You said, "No." How can I trust You ever again? What do I do with these unwept tears? The way I feel, these tears should be flowing fiercely and constantly. I guess they are sometimes stifled by the shock that he is gone from me. The sadness smothers me. I lay in my bed in the fetal position. I guess my body knows that I am about to be born yet again. Only this time into a world without the part of my heart that has mattered most. How Lord will You fill this void? Wait Lord! This void that I feel, I don't want filled. This void I feel is all I have left of him. Abba Father in times past, You came down, drew me out of many waters, and took me into Your care. This time, all Your waves and billows have truly gone over me. I am drowning in the pain of this loss. Father, You disappointed me, and still somewhere deep within me I knew that my help could only come from You. My prayer comes to You in a whisper—a single word, "Help."

Those first moments, days, weeks and months, I was not quite sure You were holding me. However, I knew Your power, compassion, empathy, and love would someday lead to my healing. I knew in my head, but my heart would not, could not, accept those truths. As time moved on, Your faithfulness slowly but surely became evident. In Your great faithfulness, You gradually brought me to the place where I could hear You again. You said to be patient with You and with myself, and so I was patient. I knew, even though I could not feel it, You were working in me and for me. You kept reminding me not to fear the darkness. The light and the darkness are both alike to You. Abba Father, keep reminding me that You hold the strength to bring me through this dark place—through this all-consuming pain, sadness, depression and hopelessness. Keep reminding me to trust You beyond logic and reason. Keep reminding me of Who You are to me and who I am to You. You are my loving Father. You are my healer. You are my very present help. You will never leave me or forsake me. You are my strength. You have all power in Your hands. You know what this is like. You gave Your Son to die so that those who mourn can continue to live even after death. Help me. Heal me. Restore the hope—that confident expectation that has brought me through hard times before.

Father, the truth is that You have been healing me all along. You have been working in me both to will and to act on Your good pleasure, to put my hope in You again and to trust You again. Thank You Father for the work I can now see You are doing in me. Now, Abba Father, give me the desire to go beyond this place of just existing. Empower me to want to live again, to thrive again!

He had always been Yours Lord. You gifted him to me for what continues to feel like way too short of a time. Then, You took him home. I know this life will never be the same. I'm coming to realize I will never be the same. I have been marred in Your (The Potter) hands. You are using what feels like evil for my good and for Your glory. This season of grief is a season of You forming me into another vessel as seems best to You. You are allowing me to go through this crucible of grief for reasons I cannot fully comprehend. Yet, I know, understand, and believe that I am seeing through a glass darkly. I know, understand, and believe that Your ways are past finding out.

Abba Father, take all my disappointment, disillusionment, and discouragement. Help me to believe that within this grace in which I stand, there is everything I need. I will know Your healing. I will know a hope that can only come from Your Holy Spirit's work in me. Help me to know You more intimately through this grief, this flip side of love. The presence of grief and absence of love cannot coexist. Strengthen my resolve to live a more meaningful and full life in and for You. Help me to embrace this newness of who I am and how I understand the world because of my loss. Help me to understand that it is okay to be broken. Help me to remember that my extremity is Your opportunity to move me toward the places You ordained for me before I was conceived.

Thank You for transporting me to a higher place of faith. Thank You for helping me to know that my pain is not in vain. Thank You for the comfort of Your loving kindness You provide to me. You were there all the time!

It is in that name that is above every name, Jesus, that I pray, amen!

Sister Roxanne Young

Sarasota, FL

My Personal Prayer of Comfort

Dear Father,

_____

_____

_____

_____

_____

_____

_____

_____

_____

Inspirational Thought:

Meditate on this... God is there to bring you comfort and strength. You are not facing this loss alone. Let this Psalm of David echo through your soul, *"Yea though I walk through the valley of the shadow of death, I will fear no evil, for Thy art with me: Thy rod and Thy staff they comfort me."* Psalm 23:4

Strength for the Weak

"But He said to me, "My grace is sufficient for you, for My power is made perfect in weakness. Therefore, I will boast all the more gladly of my weaknesses, so that the power of Christ may rest upon me. For the sake of Christ then, I am content with weaknesses, insults, hardships, persecutions, and calamities. For when I am weak, then I am strong."
2 Corinthians 12:9-10

Oh Holy and most gracious heavenly Father, I thank You Lord for being my strength and my Redeemer. You are mighty and loving. You are so faithful. Because of You, I can stand despite those things that come against me. Father, when I need strength, I lean upon Your Word that assures me that no weapon formed against me shall prosper. When the enemy comes up against me to discourage me and to weaken me in the faith, Your power helps me and Your Word encourages me and makes me strong. I am strong in You and wonderfully and fearfully made by You. I am not weak or helpless; but, I can do all things through You Who gives me strength. Thank You Father for helping me not to see myself as puny and powerless, fragile and frail – second guessing and questioning myself. I am grateful God that by Your Spirit, I am seeing a different me—one that is strong and empowered. You are the lifter of my head. You uphold me and carry me in Your loving arms. Tears I cried in my weak moments have turned into tears of joy because You helped me to be resilient. You showed me tests and trials only come to make me strong.

Lord, thank You for showing me I do not have to carry my burdens alone, being crushed under the weight of them. But, I can cast them all on You, completely Lord. You are my support. You are my strength. Even now, I lean upon You Lord and I hear You whispering, "Trust Me daughter with all your heart and lean not to your own understanding; in all your ways acknowledge Me and I will direct your path." I find strength in Your whispers and in knowing I do not have to carry these burdens alone or handle life's situations on my own.

Father, I am not weak and powerless. By faith, I declare I am strong. I am empowered by You. Glory to God! You are my help! I put all my trust in You, Oh Lord. I wait on You to renew my strength. Cause me to mount up on wings as an eagle. Help me to run and not be weary and to walk and not faint. Thank You, Lord for making me strong. You are my help, my power, my might, and my strength in Jesus' name. Amen!

Sister Daphnee Bennett-Jolley
Fragrance of Faith Ministry, Inc
Baltimore, MD

My Personal Prayer for Strength

Dear Father,

_____

_____

_____

_____

_____

_____

_____

_____

_____

_____

_____

Inspirational Thought:

Your change starts with your confession. Let the weak say, "I am strong."

Prayer for the Weak and Infirmed

"In the day when I cried out, You answered me,
And made me bold with strength in my soul."
Psalm 138:3

Lord, I give You praise for Your great compassion and Your loving kindness. You are so mindful of us and You care about us in every way. There is nothing concerning our lives that is hid from You. You know every one of our conditions, and You are faithful to help us in our times of need. Lord, there are many in this world who need You. Hear our cry oh Lord. Hear the cries of the infirmed, the sorrowful, the scorned, the alienated, the emotionally distressed, and the aggrieved. Lord heal wounded hearts and minds that have been traumatized by life's situations. Gird up the loins of our minds. Strengthen us. Let us not buckle under the pressures of life. Renew our confidence, Oh Lord. Replace feelings of insecurity, vulnerability, anxiety, and hopelessness with courage, hope, optimism, and a deep faith in You.

Heal bodies Lord that have been impacted by acts of violence, physical ordeals, and the stressors of life. Let the physically infirmed receive ongoing comfort and relief to every organ and limb. Oh great Physician, regenerate nerve endings, restore red blood cells, and fortify white blood cells, capillaries, corpuscles, and platelets in the name of Jesus. Heal every area of our bodies—muscles, skeletal tissues, tendons, ligaments, and gelatinous materials. Regulate and refresh our bodies, so the sick will be healed and rise up and give You glory. You are a Sovereign Salve, Oh Lord. Bolster our bodies with renewed energy and motivate our spirit to align with Your will, in Jesus name!

Holy Spirit, let us not be discouraged in whatsoever state we find ourselves because You are our help. Lord, help us to hear Your voice so that our doubts and fears are destroyed. Father, fortify our minds, and quicken our spirit that we may receive the truth and act upon it. Increase our faith by undergirding us with Your wisdom, peace, and love that all negative words or thoughts intended to destroy us are taken captive by Your mighty Word. Your Word declares we are the apple of Your eye, which speaks of the depth of Your love for us. Lord, we know that You will be our help. Holy Spirit, breathe on us! Invigorate us! Let the power of Your passion quicken our spirit and give us hope! We yearn for Your healing power, and we receive it right now in Jesus' name!

We are no longer weak and feeble, distraught and distressed. But we are the healed of the Lord and the righteousness of Christ Jesus. Thank You for establishing us, healing us, and making us complete, entire, and lacking nothing so that we can do Your will and good pleasure. Thank You for reviving our souls. Thank You for alleviating our burdens as we cast all our cares upon You. Thank You for granting us rest and hope. Thank You for taking away our weariness and our weakness. Thank You for not leaving us in the bondage of brokenness and in our downtrodden state. Thank You for the power of Your love that lifts us up to higher ground. Thank You for Your love that is restorative, reinvigorating, and responsive to our every need. Thank You for choosing to heal us, and strengthen us so that You can ultimately use us for Your glory and praise. You are no respecter of person. You have chosen the weak to confound the wise. We bless Your name!

God, we thank You for restored health, joy, and peace. Help us to remember that we do not have to stay burdened down. We do not have to stay weak, wounded, and afflicted in our souls, minds, and bodies. But Lord, You our healer will give us beauty for our ashes. You will be our strength. For this cause, You died for us to make us whole. Thank You! Thank You for Your Spirit Who lives on the inside of us, always reminding us that we have the victory in Christ Jesus. We declare victory over every weakness and infirmity, in Jesus' name. Amen.

Reverend Tanya A. Smith
Providence Baptist Church of San Francisco
San Francisco, CA

My Personal Prayer for the Weak and Infirmed

Dear Father,

_____

_____

_____

_____

_____

_____

_____

Inspirational Thought:

"God is our refuge and strength, A very present help in trouble. Therefore, will not we fear, though the earth be removed, And, though the mountains be carried into the midst of the sea. Though the waters thereof roar and be troubled, though the mountains shake with the swelling thereof. There is a river, the streams whereof shall make glad the city of God, the holy place of the tabernacles of the Most High." Psalm 46:1-4

Healing for the Sick

"And the prayer of faith shall save the sick, and the LORD shall raise him up; and if he has committed sins, they shall be forgiven him"

James 5:15

Jehovah-Rapha, the LORD our Healer, it is in the name of Jesus Christ, we Your people called by Your name, pause to pray. We come seeking Your face, taking nothing for granted. We pray about the weariness, the sicknesses, the illnesses and the diseases in the earth. We prayer cover our lives, our health and well-being. We look unto the hills from where our help comes from. Our faith looks up because we recognize our help comes from You Lord, the Maker of heaven and earth. Our need for You is greater than we can articulate. You are an awesome Wonder, the great I Am. There is none like You! You are able to help, heal, save, and deliver.

God, so many need You. Even at this very hour—those in nursing homes, hospitals and hospice; those on life support and ventilators; those going in surgery and coming out of surgery; those in recovery and those in rehabilitation—all need You. Send Your healing power Lord. Heal the cancer patient, the heart patient, the kidney patient, the stroke patient, the critically ill patient, and all those battling with infirmities. We call forth what is needed for wellness, wholeness and healing. Strengthen our weak places. Make us strong in the power of Your might. Let Your Word work on our behalf touching every ailment. Let Your Word become flesh. Let it get down into the marrow, bones, joints, cells, muscles, tissues, nerves, vessels, and in the blood stream. Dear Jesus, minister to our bodies. Stretch forth Your healing hand. Annihilate ailments, heal hurts, abolish aches, squash sickness, and destroy death, depression, and diseases from our bodies. Let medicine work! Let medical procedures work! Let medical advice work! Most of all, let Your Word be at work in us. Send Your Word Lord to heal us! Your Word will not return back unto You void.

God, Your Word tells us that You wish above all things that we prosper and be in good health. Your Word tells us that healing is the children's bread. Your Word tells us that if You heal us, we shall be healed. Heal our blindness, heal our lameness, heal our brokenness, heal our issues, and heal our lifelessness. Jesus, call our bodies into order. Have mercy upon us according to Thy loving kindness and Thy tender mercies. Make us physically and mentally whole. We ask You Lord to blot out our transgressions and wash us thoroughly from our iniquities. Create in us a clean heart and renew a right spirit within us. Revive us again. Restore our health. Send a cure and let the prayer of faith heal us.

God, just as Hezekiah did, we turn our face to the wall. Heal our wounds and extend our years. Speak life over our lives. God put Your Super on our natural. Shift the atmosphere. Bring Your healing, miraculous power in our midst. We are standing on Your promises, and believe You to be the Miracle Worker Who will heal every sickness. We beseech You to heal us now. By Your stripes, heal us! By Your blood, heal us! By Your Word, heal us! By Your Spirit, heal us! By Your Power, heal us! Let healing be manifested in every area of our lives. Heal our wounds; heal our scars; heal our broken hearts; heal our souls. Heal us emotionally Lord. Remove rage, harshness, and haughtiness. Help us to relax in You and walk in humility. God make our bodies, minds, and spirit healthy. Destroy dementia, annihilate Alzheimer, halt headaches, and transform our thoughts. Jesus, do more than we can ask or think.

Lord, heal the back slider, and heal our land. Heal our families—our marriages, our children, and our parents. Heal our communities. Heal our churches. Stretch forth Your hands oh Lord. Release wellness. Let it spring forth like the noon day! Make every crooked place straight, every rough place smooth, and every bitter place sweet. God, we call those things that be not as though they are. We trust You and lean not to our own understanding. Our faith looks up to Thee, oh Lamb of God. You can do all things but fail. Let our faith please You, and let the prayer of faith heal us in Jesus' name we pray. Amen.

Maxine Rush
Shiloh Baptist Church of Baltimore County
Edgemere, MD

My Personal Prayer for Healing

Dear Father,

_____

_____

_____

_____

_____

_____

_____

_____

_____

_____

Inspirational Thought:

"Behold, I will bring to it health and healing, and I will heal them and reveal to them abundance of prosperity and security."
Jeremiah 33:6. Give God the praise! He has a plan for your life. Sickness is not the end of your story. Get ready for an abundance of blessings!

A Prayer for Our Nation

"After this manner therefore pray ye: Our Father which art in heaven, Hallowed be Thy name. Thy kingdom come, Thy will be done in earth, as it is in heaven. Give us this day our daily bread. And forgive us our debts, as we forgive our debtors. And lead us not into temptation, but deliver us from evil: For Thine is the kingdom, and the power, and the glory, forever."
Matthew 6:9-13

Lord, we pray our Father Who art in heaven let your name be hallowed throughout the nations. Let everything that have breath give You praise!

Father, we thank You for hearing our prayers as we pause to pray for our nation. We need You in every area of our nation and in so many ways. Let Your kingdom come, and let Your will be done in our homes, in our communities, on our jobs, in the marketplace, in our businesses, and in our governments. Let Your will be done in our schools and in our universities where our children need to be taught according to the laws of Your kingdom. Lord, show up in all of these places and correct the wrong and fix the broken.

Lord, we pray for protection over our nation. Cover our nation and cover our borders from the enemy. Lord, let the atmosphere of heaven be released into the air, the water, the soil, and in the food to protect us from the things we cannot protect ourselves from. Let heaven release that which will destroy chemicals, bacteria, viruses, and any plague that threatens the lives of all people around the world. Lord, cover us.

Father, we pray for those in our country who are in need of food, raiment, and resources. Holy Father, give us this day our daily bread. Let the spirit of giving be released upon the nation. Give us a heart for those who are suffering during these troubled times. Father, many have lost their jobs and the ability to care for their families. They need help. Lord, give us eyes to see, ears to hear, and hearts to move on the desperate cries of the people in the land. Lord Jesus, You said the works You did, we would do also and even greater because You went to the Father. So prepare us to multiply the little that we have to become much in Your hands. Let miracles, signs, and wonders be released around the world so the needs of the people will be met.

Lord, we pray for a sound to be released in the nation. We pray that the people of the nation will cry out to You according to Psalm 107, *"Then they cried unto the Lord in their trouble, and He delivered them out of their distresses."* Hear the cries of Your people Lord, and save them from calamity and death. For You are a merciful, God, not willing that any should perish. *"O give thanks unto the Lord, for He is good: for His mercy endureth for ever."* (Psalm 107:1).

Then Lord, we pray for a spirit of forgiveness to be released in this nation and even abroad. Help us to forgive those who have offended us, deceived us, betrayed us, and committed unspeakable violations against us. Let nations forgive other nations and bring healing across the land. Let forgiveness be released in our families, to our co-workers, to our friends, and others who we may be holding un-forgiveness towards. We want pure hearts before You God. Lord, we pray for a righteous nation.

Father, please do not allow us to be tempted above our ability to overcome the temptation. Deliver us from all evil known and unknown. Protect every dimensional access point that the enemy would try to use to infiltrate our nation and launch an attack against us. Protect our nation by deploying angels around our borders. God, let billions of angels be deployed throughout the entire planet. Let the angels war in the spirit realm against the fallen angels and their army. Let them release Your wrath, division, strife, contention, and confusion, Lord, upon the kingdom of darkness, that Your kingdom will come in the earth and prevail. Let the kingdoms of this world become the kingdoms of our God. God, we even pray for the human agents of darkness who have been deceived by Satan to do evil; block them Lord, and bring them to repentance. Save their very souls.

Now Lord, let the nations release an atmosphere of praise around the world, inviting You to dwell among us. Give us a longing to fellowship with Your Holy Spirit. Deliver us from our finite understanding of Who You are to the nations. Help us to understand that You are God, God over all, and Your yearning was so intense for the world You sent Your only begotten Son to give His life for us. You love us so. We are Your creation, and You long for a genuine relationship and fellowship with us. Show us how to draw nearer to You so that You can fulfill Your promise to draw near to us. We love You, Lord. Bless our nation. In Jesus' name. Amen

Karen Brown
Campaign for Souls
Middletown, DE

My Personal Prayer for the Nation

Dear Father,

_____

_____

_____

_____

_____

_____

_____

_____

Inspirational Thought:

"Bless the Lord, O my soul and all that is within me, bless His Holy name. Bless the Lord, O my soul, and forget not all His benefits: Who forgiveth all thine iniquities; Who healeth all thy diseases; Who redeemeth thy life from destruction; Who crowneth thee with loving kindness and tender mercies." Psalm 103:1-4

Prayer for Justice in Our Nation

"The LORD is our God bringing justice everywhere on earth."
Psalms 105:7

Oh Lord, our Lord, how excellent is Your name in all the earth and greatly to be praised. We enter into Your gates with thanksgiving and into Your courts with praise. You are high and lifted up with all our adoration and praise. We worship and bless You for Your everlasting love, peace, grace, and mercy towards us. We are in awe of You! Your awesomeness and faithfulness amaze us, and endure forever to all generations. You are the Holy and Majestic One, the Righteous Judge in Whom we call on now. We come before Your mighty throne of grace with humbled hearts and contrite spirits. We need You Lord, God.

We are calling on Your name and seeking Your face for justice in our nation, the United States of America. We pray Your kingdom come and Your will be done to reverse the spirit of injustice that is running rampant in our land. Lord, bind up the enemy who seeks to divide and devour Your people with fear, racism, prejudices, and biases. Lord, move on the hearts and minds of people across our cities and states who are guilty of doing wrong to others and operating in wicked, evil, and unjust practices causing innocent lives to be destroyed. Many have suffered unjustly and have also been incarcerated unfairly. God expose and eradicate any discriminatory legal systems, judiciary practices, and agendas which target the innocent. Righteous Judge, bring vindication for all those who have been or are being wrongly prosecuted and persecuted. Reveal any subversive and covet agendas that are waged against Your people to oppress them. Lord Your people who are called by Your name, who love You, and seek to do Your will above all else ask that You cover us from all injustice and let Your justice prevail and ring throughout all the land.

Dear God, we declare we will see You moving in our government, in our judicial system, and in our cities and states like never before— eradicating what does not belong. Spirit of the living God, bring forth Your Light into the dark places of our land—in our government, in our judicial and educational system, and in our institutions. God, remove any judge from their chamber who refuses to operate in ethical practices, free of discrimination and biases. Whether it is in the highest court—the Supreme Court, the district court, or down to the local court, please remove them. Father, release a fresh wind of God-fearing wisdom, prudence, and fairness in the legal system of this land so that it may impact lawyers, police officers, city officials, and all who exercise laws and rule over us. Set the captives free of those who were falsely imprisoned and give them restitution like only You can.

Dear Lord, bring conviction in the heart of anyone, anywhere who operates out of hatred, jealousy, envy, strife, and deception—going along with all manner of sin, unjustly attacking, killing, and destroying others, wreaking mayhem. Father, break the strongholds off their life and deliver them from being a puppet of the enemy. Bring them out of darkness and into Your marvelous Light. Help them to love, live justly, and walk uprightly.

God, we thank You for restoring righteousness. Let Your law and order return in our nation. You said in Your Word, *"Righteousness exalts a nation, but sin condemns any people."* (Proverbs 14:34). Father, we declare our nation to be righteous, where Your justice prevails. By the power and authority of the blood of Jesus, we decree, declare, and believe justice is being upheld everywhere in this land. Chains are being broken, the oppressed are being raised up, and victories are breaking forth for those who have been underserved and misrepresented. The Word of God is manifesting in the land, civility and justice are being restored, hearts and minds are being turned to God, and the love of Jesus is being shown. Like the dawning of a new day, change is springing forth for the glory of God!

Now Lord, for Your children who have decided to live for You, help us to defend justice and advocate for Your righteousness by having nothing to do with the fruitless deeds of darkness. Quicken our spirit to operate with spiritual discernment, courage, and strength so that we can stand up with a righteous indignation to expose and rebuke wrong doings. Help us to speak out when we see injustice in our midst. We want to be good witnesses and ambassadors of righteousness for Your glory, honor, and praise.

We thank You God for inclining Your ear to our prayer and granting us the supplication of our hearts. We pray for healing and blessings upon the United States of America. We love, honor, and bless You, in the mighty name of Jesus, Amen!

Sister Brenda Gibbs
Calvary Gospel Church
Waldorf, MD

My Personal Prayer for God's Justice in the Nation

Dear Father,

_____

_____

_____

_____

_____

_____

_____

_____

Inspirational Thought:

Do not worry. Just do good and love justice. Be fair and show the love of Jesus to all mankind. The Lord will handle everything concerning you. _"Fret not thyself because of evildoers, neither be thou envious against the workers of iniquity. For they shall soon be cut down like the grass, and wither as the green herb. Trust in the LORD, and do good; so shalt thou dwell in the land, and verily thou shalt be fed."_ Psalms 37:1-3.

A Prayer for Justice in the World

"This is what the LORD Almighty said: Administer true justice; show mercy and compassion to one another."
Zechariah 7:9

Heavenly Father, I know You are a God of justice. You see everything that has taken place in this world, and You are acting on it! There is nothing that escapes You. Your eyes go to and fro in the earth beholding the good and the evil. God, You know the unjust, unfair, and ruthless acts of mankind against the marginalized. We align ourselves with heaven's agenda and take back everything that has been stolen through the injustice of others. As Your mighty warriors and more than conquerors, we put on the whole armor of God, and apply the blood of Jesus Christ for our protection as we go in and pray for justice and against the deeds of darkness. We decree, absolutely nothing shall be able to harm us.

Now Holy Spirit, we welcome You to empower us to bring the will of God into the earth and into our justice system. You are the Rock we stand upon while advancing this prayer, and the gates of hell will not prevail against us. Thank You for downloading strategies and teaching us how to wield our swords to make a difference in this world. Father God, by faith, we are here to pray in the Spirit what we desire to see manifested in the natural. We are here to contend for justice and will not give up or give in until change happens. Hear our prayers oh Lord. We shut down the plans in this world's systems that promote wickedness and oppression. We serve notice on the enemy to go NOW! In Jesus' name!

We cast out the spirits of leviathan, narcissism, entitlement, racism, pride, mammon, abuse, and all things that work against justice. We forbid injustice in our land. We forbid the enemy from operating in our judicial and educational systems, in our government and in every institution that has been established to serve the needs of the people. We cancel the plans of the enemy, in Jesus name. Lord, You are a consuming fire. Burn up plans that are unjust and unfair. Burn up plans that do not consider the poor, the needy, the downtrodden, and the disenfranchised.

God, You are Jehovah Tsaba, the Lord Our Warrior and El Shaddai, God Almighty. We know You will fight for us. Your Word tells us in Exodus 15:3 *"The Lord is a warrior, the Lord is His name."* God, we pray You will war on the behalf of Your people so that they are not mistreated or harmed by the discriminatory practices and acts of men. Lord, teach us to war and our fingers to do battle. Even now, we cut off the head of every perverted system that is not balanced or equal for all and that has built in wickedness and biases. We pray every authority, every leader, and every person in power will operate in a fair and just manner in the affairs of Your people.

We come at an accelerated pace, in the name of the Lord of Host, to recover what was stolen from those who have been dealt with unfairly and unjustly. We pray Your mercy to a thousand generations. Let every prisoner go from the grip of oppressive acts and unfair treatment. We declare they are set free in Jesus' name. God, we enforce Your justice and recompense on every victim that has been taken advantage of and mishandled.

God, even as we pray for justice, we pray for our judicial system that was supposed to represent justice for all. But God, as You know, through the years it has truly fallen short of its responsibility. There have been so much corruption and unfairness. So right now, we dismiss every corrupt police officer, judge, lawyer, court-appointed clerk, prosecutor, and interrogator. Send them to their knees. Provoke them to repentance of their wickedness and the harm they have caused others. Let none escape. We declare conviction upon their hearts. Visit each one who has caused pain upon prisoners, foster children, juvenile detainees, and such. Bring them to their knees. Show up in their dreams, homes, jobs, vehicles, everywhere they go. Let them hear the footsteps of a mighty army pursuing them. We pray You reveal the cross to them and they see Jesus face to face. May they be wrecked by Your love according to Your Word in John 3:16 that lets us know, You so love us all. Whatever ties they have with wickedness, we break them off of them and detach them from evil. Let them receive the truth that sets them free. Remove the stony hearts, and give them hearts of flesh so that they can show love and treat others with kindness and fairness. Change their very demeanor and their behavior so that they will be pleasing unto You. God, those who refuse to change and continue to act with cruelty and prejudices, we pray You will remove them from their seats of authority and influence.

Lord, we come on the behalf of the people. Let Your kingdom come and Your will be done on earth as it is in heaven. Let Your agenda supersede the agenda of the oppressors and may the oppressors turn to Your righteousness. Lord, we pray for the justice system to go through a massive transformation. We pray You will raise up righteous men and women to take over our judicial system. And Lord, we pray for those righteous men and women of God who presently work in the judicial systems, that they will have courage and boldness to stand up for what is right and to defend the defenseless. Let them see there are more with them than are against them, and that they are not alone in their fight for justice. In Jesus mighty name!

Finally, Lord, we pray for the rehabilitation and restoration to individuals and families who have been victims of an unjust judicial system. God restore those who have been falsely accused, falsely incarcerated, and abused by the system. Restore them emotionally, physically, and financially. Make them complete and whole. Let all things work together for their good. For all the years they were without, we declare a 100-fold blessing in their lives. For their shame, we declare double honor. Restore their name. Open doors for them that no man can shut. Give them a mindset to rise up from their oppression and thrive. We pray new businesses, innovative ideas, inventions, and careers to emerge. May each one who has been victimized emerge from the rubble of their pain—painful words, and painful events. Though they have gone through difficult times, God let them know You did not forget them and You have a plan to restore their dignity and help them to recoup their losses. Heal them from their trauma. Give their lives meaning and purpose. Restore their dreams. Repay them double for their trouble.

Father God, we care about what You care about, and we hate what You hate. We know You care about justice and You hate injustice. Let us forever pray to see a turnaround and pray that our world will begin to look different. Let us see more love for one another with an understanding that we are all Your creation, made in Your image and in Your likeness. God, we thank You that no one has superiority over another based upon their race, creed, color, or class. Every knee will bow and every tongue will confess Jesus that You are Lord.

We pray and believe by faith this prayer is gone forth with signs and wonders following. In Jesus' mighty name. Amen!

Minister Tammy Smith
Speak Life Ministry of Virginia
Newport News, VA

My Personal Prayer for Justice in the World

Dear Father,

_____

_____

_____

_____

_____

_____

_____

_____

_____

_____

Inspirational Thought:

When you are the victim of injustice, racism, biases and unfair treatment, it can be painful and sometimes leave you wanting to take revenge. But don't! God's got this. This is what He says to you... "*Dearly beloved, avenge not yourselves, but rather give place unto wrath: for it is written, Vengeance is Mine; I will repay, saith the Lord.*" Romans 12:19.

Direction and Guidance

"Commit everything you do to the Lord, Trust Him, and He will help you."
Psalm 37:5

Heavenly Father, we bow down before You, lifting our hearts unto You. We thank You for being our Counselor, our way maker, and our guide. Lord, we seek Your face in everything we do. You are Abba Father, and we stand in need of Your guidance and Your direction on this journey called life. Every step we make, Lord go ahead of us. Cover our every move, in Jesus name.

Lord, as it concerns our health, guide us for we know You want us to be in good health as stated in Your Word, *"Beloved, I wish above all things that thou mayest prosper and be in health, even as thy soul prospereth".* (3 John 1:3). Lord, we stand on Your Word and ask that You will lead us in optimum health. Bless every organ, cell, muscle, and bone so they will operate the way You have designed for them to function. Lead us away from those things which are detrimental to our health, causing harm to our bodies and mind. Give us Your wisdom as we seek You for guidance to walk in divine health throughout our days and our years. Let us receive Your God given wisdom to walk in wellness and wholeness. We praise Your great name and thank You for good health in Jesus' name.

Lord, as it concerns our peace, we thank You for guiding us into the way of peace. Your Word tells us, *"And the peace of God which passes all understanding, will guard your hearts and your minds in Christ Jesus."* (Philippians 4:7). Thank You God for Your peace in a world with many challenges. We thank You for removing anything that comes as a distraction to upset us, frustrate us, and thus hinder us from living out our purpose. Let us not be moved; but, keep our hearts at ease and our eyes fixed on You. Bless us with calm spirits and restful hearts having a full assurance that You are leading us and guiding us in the way we should go. You are right here to help us. We thank You Lord that in these tumultuous times, You guide our feet into the way of peace. Let the peace of God rule our hearts and direct our path. Let it be the very compass of our way.

Daddy, we thank You for not only guiding us and leading us into the place of peace, but for also leading us into a place of safety. Psalm 4:6 says, *"In peace I will lie down and sleep, for You alone, Lord, make me dwell in safety."* Lord, we look to You for our safety. Keep us safe from dangers seen and unseen. Keep us safe from violence, viruses, natural disasters, terrorist attacks, and untimely deaths. Lord, help us to be vigilant and mindful of our surroundings. Give us a clear mind so we can hear Your voice as You direct our feet into safety. Father, we trust You to steer danger away from our dwelling place. God, You are in control and we thank You in Jesus name!

Father, we also thank You for directing us as it concerns our careers and those things that we aspire to do and be. God Your Word says in Psalm 37:4, *"Delight yourself in the Lord, and He will give you the desires of your heart."* Lord, even as we delight in serving You, worshiping You, and praying to You, please grant us the desires of our hearts. Direct us on the right career path, the right occupation, and the right business. Give us the desires of our hearts so that we will desire what You desire for our lives. Then Lord, please show us how to lay hold of those desires and be faithful unto You Who placed them in our hearts. Let our performance align with Your will, and help us to follow You explicitly so we can flourish, grow, expand, and multiply. Help us to follow Your principles, trusting You will provide everything we need to be successful.

We thank You Father for Your wisdom and guidance. We believe You will lead us concerning all these things that we have laid before You: our health, our peace, our safety, our careers, and all of our endeavors. Let Your Holy Spirit give us fresh revelation of Your will. We only want to hear Your voice in these matters. Let Your voice orchestrate and direct our feet for Your name sake. Then Lord, give us God wisdom, knowledge, and understanding to abide in Your way. We stand on Proverbs 3:5-6, that says... *"Trust in the Lord with all thine heart; and lean not unto thine own understanding. In all thy ways acknowledge Him, and He shall direct thy paths."* Glory to God! Thank You Father for directing our paths into God-ordained and God-blessed places and situations. In Jesus' name we pray. Amen

Sister Kathy Wells
Shiloh Baptist Church of Baltimore County
Elkridge, MD

My Personal Prayer for Direction and Guidance

Dear Father,

_____

_____

_____

_____

_____

_____

_____

_____

_____

_____

_____

Inspirational Thought:

"Commit to the Lord whatever you do, and He will establish your plans. The LORD works out everything to its proper end..."
Proverbs 16:3-4. Let the Lord be your guide.

Lord Lead Us, Guide Us

"Trust in the Lord with all your heart, and lean not on your own understanding; In all your ways acknowledge Him, and He shall direct your paths."
Proverbs 3:5-6

Father God, we exalt Your Holy name. We reverence Your presence and we thank You for Your abundant grace toward us. We look to the hills from where our help comes, knowing our help comes from You, the Maker of heaven and earth. We confidently come before You to pray for direction and guidance in our lives.

Lord, we are at a place in our lives where we do not know what to do or which way to go. We seek You for divine wisdom, discernment, clarity and understanding. God, You know the way we should take. Lord, show us the course You have charted for our lives and give us the faith to walk therein. We seek You for direction and guidance for each new day because we do not want to navigate through life without Your blueprint. We seek to do Your will. We seek after You. Holy Spirit, be our guide. Order our steps in Your Word and be the compass for our way. The scripture tells us, *"Your Word is a lamp unto [our] feet and a light unto [our] path."* (Psalm 119:105). We are grateful for Your Word and we desperately need Your Light to guide our feet on this journey called life. It is our hearts' desire to follow after You. We want Your guidance in every area of our lives.

God, we want to hear Your voice as it concerns our families. Show us how to take care of them—how to lead, protect, and build our love ones up to be strong in You. Lord, we also ask that You show us how to nurture healthy and positive relationships with family and friends. Show us how to go about repairing the fractures in our relationships. Lead us and guide us on the road of forgiveness and help us to show the love of God. Guide us into the way of peace. Let us be led by peace in our decision making and in our interaction with man.

Then Lord, show us how to develop and grow on our jobs, in our careers, and in our business ventures. We want to maximize every opportunity and increase in every potential. You know the gifts, the talent, and the skills You have deposited in us. Lord, orchestrate divine encounters and connections on our jobs and in our careers whereby we can utilize what You have placed on the inside of us to bless others to for Your honor, glory, and praise.

Lord, we call out to You to direct our path and to order our steps in these areas of our lives so that we may prosper and be in good health (physically, mentally and emotionally) even as our soul prospers. Shine Your Light around us and lead us in the paths of righteousness for Your name sake. We decree and declare, we will not be led astray! We will not be deterred by the enemy and his tactics to shift our focus on his plan that leads to darkness and destruction. Nor will we set out on our own path, setting our own course. But, God our eyes are fixed upon You. You are our Lamp Who lightens our way and Who ushers us on to victory. There is no failure when we are led by the Light of Your glory.

We rise up dear God and by Your power, we bind every spirit of confusion, chaos, anxiety, and fear about our future or the path we should take. *"For [You] hath not given us the spirit of fear; but of power, and of love, and of a sound mind."* (2 Timothy 1:7). We will not be intimidated by the enemy to forge ahead, even into the unknown, the place where You are leading. We trust in You God. Thank You Lord we can rest in knowing that You have a sure mapped out plan for our lives. You will instruct and teach us in the way we should go. You will guide us with Your eyes and Your finger of love! Glory to Your name Jesus! We put our faith in You and believe in Your Word that declares, *"Trust in the LORD with all thine heart; And lean not unto thine own understanding. In all thy ways acknowledge Him, And He shall direct thy paths."* Lord, with all our hearts, we acknowledge You, and believe and trust that You will direct our path. Holy Spirit, align our thoughts with Your thoughts and our ways with Your ways. May our ears always be open to hear and adhere to Your voice for Your Word declares, *"Whether you turn to the right or to the left, your ears will hear a voice behind you, saying 'This is the way; walk in it."* Glory to God! Your Word will declare unto us, "This is the way; walk in it"! Lord, I have set You before me. I see a clear path. Hallelujah!

Lord, as we seek to do what is perfect in Your sight, thank You for Your patience and compassion. We thank You for taking the time to correct us and to show us the way. You will set our course. Blessed are all those who put their trust in You and wait for You! We find comfort in knowing You have set all things in order. We release all anxiety, fear, confusion, worry, and frustration. We walk in peace with full assurance that You will give us clear direction and divine guidance on our journey. We thank You, In Jesus' name. Amen

Sister Kimberly R. Alcorn
Haymarket, VA

My Personal Prayer for God to Lead and Guide

Dear Father,

_____

_____

_____

_____

_____

_____

_____

_____

_____

_____

_____

Inspirational Thought:

If you will let Him, God will lead you. Let His Word be a lamp unto your feet and a light unto your path.

Prayer for Peace

"And the peace of God, which passeth all understanding, shall keep your hearts and minds through Christ Jesus."
Philippians 4:7

Abba Father, we hallow Your name. We give You praise for You are our God, the Holy One. You are Alpha and Omega, the Beginning and the End, and we bless You. God thank You that You already know what we need and You will hear us when we call.

God, we come seeking peace because we live in a world that has been shaken and people are unsettled. Jeremiah 29:7 lets us know that we can seek the peace of our cities. We need Your peace across every region and territory. Let Your peace overshadow and surround our cities. Father God, we know that You are able to bring peace in every chaotic place and in every troubled place in our world and in our hearts. You are the embodiment of peace. You are the peace that we seek. You are Jehovah Shalom, the Almighty God, the Prince of Peace. Lord, we seek Your peace across the land for Your people. Give us a calm and a resolve. Cause violence, hatred, contention, strife, anxiety and fear to cease; and let Your peace flow from the east coast to the west coast and from the north to the south.

Lord, let Your peace that passes all understanding rule our hearts. Let it flow Lord, let it flow, like a mighty stream of water refreshing our souls. God, You have ordained peace for Your people; so, let Your peace saturate our atmosphere filling our mind, body, soul, and spirit. Guide our feet into the way of peace, making our enemies to be at peace with us. Praise You the God of Peace. Oh how we praise You!

God, Prince of Peace, grant us Your peace like no one else can. Just as the mountains surround Jerusalem, let Your peace surround our minds. Let us not act out of impulse, fear, or anxiety. Help us not to be worried and shaken by what we see and what we hear. But let Your very presence give us the assurance we need, settling our hearts, calming our fears, and soothing all of our doubts. Help us to keep our minds stayed on You because You promised that if we would keep our minds on You, You would keep us in perfect peace.

God, even now, our minds are fixed upon You: upon Your goodness, Your mercies, and Your grace. We think on those things that are lovely, pure, of a good report, and of praise unto You. So God, where we are unsettled, settle us. Where we are worried, walk with us. Where we are restless, give us rest to our souls knowing everything will be alright—whether in our city, in our homes, or in our hearts. You will take care of us. God help us to know, we do not have to collapse under the pressures of this world because You will be our sustaining help. You will be our peace.

Thank You Father for calming our spirits and the winds and the waves all around us, declaring to them, "Peace, be still!" Thank You God for Your peace that wipes away our worries, our fears, and our tears. We are planted in You: connected, consumed, and covered by Your divine peace. We shall not fear. We shall not be dismayed. We shall not be anxious. But, we will take refuge in You and rest in Your sovereignty. No matter what we see, we will hold onto our peace knowing that we stand on many precious promises. You are the God of Abraham, Isaac and Jacob, a covenant keeping God. You are faithful and forever just.

Father God, we bless and adore You. We give You praise! We praise You for the presence of Your peace. It is in Your Holy name, Jesus the Christ that we pray, amen.

Servant Dr. Garmi Hill- Visionary and CEO
Y'shua Ministries International
Winston-Salem, NC

My Personal Prayer for Peace

Dear Father,

_____

_____

_____

_____

_____

_____

_____

_____

_____

_____

Inspirational Thought:

If Jesus would clothe the lilies of the field, how much more would He take care of You. May the very thought of His faithfulness towards you, give you peace. *"Now the Lord of peace Himself give you peace always by all means..."* 2 Thessalonians 3:16.

God Reign in the Earth through Me

"But you will receive power when the Holy Spirit comes upon you;
and you will be My witnesses, telling people about Me everywhere –
in Jerusalem, throughout Judea, in Samaria, and to the ends of the
earth."

Acts 1:8

Dear heavenly Father, thank You for the gift of life and for the many blessings You have given me. Even more so, I want to thank You for Your Son Jesus, Your precious gift of salvation, and Your Holy Spirit within me Who leads, guides, and equips me to be light and salt in the earth.

Father, I ask that You give me a "Kingdom" mentality with the same attitude and attributes that Jesus had. Jesus' desire was to abide in You and to do Your good pleasure. He was a true servant in the earth amongst men. I want to have that kind of relationship with You Father so that Your Holy Spirit can reign in the earth through me as Your faithful servant. Use me as a vessel for Your glory so others will see the light in me that leads directly to Jesus. Help me to live out the fruit of the Spirit in my daily interactions with others so they will see You reigning in the earth and moving in their lives. Create in me a strong desire to grow in the knowledge of You, allowing Your Holy Spirit to take root in me so that I may produce much fruit that will overflow into the lives of others. Let the love and kindness I show be a representative of Your presence in the earth.

Reign in the earth Lord through me, Your servant. Reign Jesus reign! Reign through me with Your love, Your joy, Your patience, and Your kindness. Help me to love those who may not love me back; to show patience to those who are indifferent; and to show kindness to those who are not so kind. Help me to serve others, even when I may be in need so the needy will see Your loving kindness. Lord work through me; reign through me in the earth.

Father, continue to transform my mind. Make me more and more like Jesus so that I can be a suitable witness in this world and people will see You. Make me an instrument fit for Your use, walking contrary to my fleshly desires and worldly lusts. I want to be Your representative in the earth so that wherever I am, there You are performing Your wondrous acts. Let Your kingdom come, Your will be done in the earth, as it is in heaven.

Father, Your Word says, *"The eyes of the Lord run to and fro throughout the whole earth, looking to show Himself strong on behalf of those whose heart is loyal to Him"* (2 Chronicles 16:9a). Father, show Yourself strong in me that others will see You in Your splendor. Use me to cast out devils and evil spirits, and to heal the sick. Use me to shift the atmosphere, causing revivals and souls to cry out, "What must I do to be saved?" Use me to bring peace and Your goodwill in the earth. Live in me, God. Reign through me God! All these things I pray so others will say, "Truly the Lord is in this place. He reigns over all." In Jesus' mighty name I pray. Amen.

Dr. Carolane Williams, Ph.D.
Christian Life Church
Baltimore, MD

My Personal Prayer for God's Spirit to Reign through Me

Dear Father,

_____

_____

_____

_____

_____

_____

_____

_____

_____

Inspirational Thought:

You are important to God. He has need of you to be an instrument of His praise and His glory. *"Let your light shine before men, that they may see your good works and glorify the Father which is in heaven."* Matthew 5:16.

Lord, You Reign!

"The Lord reigns, He is robed in majesty; the Lord is robed in majesty and armed with strength; indeed, the world is established, firm and secure."

Psalm 93:1

Father God, we bless Your Holy name. We reverence You as our Lord and Savior! We love You with an everlasting love. We say thank You for being a faithful, loving, and kind God Who commands Your goodness to follow us and extends new mercies to us each day. Thank You Lord for being our Sovereign King Who reigns over all. You sit high, but You look down low into the earth, interceding on our behalf. For this we say, "Thank You!"

God, You are omnipresent, everywhere in the earth at the same time protecting us and protecting our families, friends, and our nation. We thank You for Your covering. You rule and reign in the earth forever and ever! Even when things seem dark and hopeless in our world, we know You are "The Great I Am" enthroned upon the circle of the earth. You are seated upon the throne, controlling the universe. From generation to generation, You have all authority, and we can put our trust in You. Just to know that You, Who have absolute power, are here in the earth taking care of us, gives us great comfort. You have not left us and would never leave us. In the face of difficulties and uncertainties, You remain, You reign, and You rule in the earth and in our lives. You have the final say in all those matters that concern us. *"For You, O Lord, are the 'Most High' over all the earth and are exalted far above all gods"* (Psalm 9:9). Hallelujah!

Father, when we are going through situations in this world—the test, the trials, and the battles of life, help us to lean not to our own understanding. Help us not to be discouraged or tied up in the bondage of fear. When our hearts are overwhelmed due to life circumstances, heartache, and pain help us to turn to You for strength and comfort knowing that You are there to help us. You are there in control reigning over all, for Your Word says, *"The Lord reigns, He is clothed with Majesty. The Lord has clothed and girded Himself with strength; Indeed, the world is firmly established, and it will not be moved."* (Psalm: 93:1). Hallelujah! You Who reign, the Supreme One, is our anchor and will cause us not to be moved! You will keep us anchored in You. Though situations are forever changing, though the earth be shaken, You are our steadfast hope. For that, we thank You Father.

Father God, we love You. We worship and adore You just for Who You are to us. We are so blessed to have a loving Father Who cares so much for His children. You hear our cries and You move on our behalf. Thank You for loving us unconditionally. Thank You for Your precious Holy Spirit Who operates in the earth. He dwells within us, always reminding us of Your power to keep us, Your faithfulness never to leave us, and Your promises towards us. Bless You Holy Spirit, You Reign in all the earth!

Father, just as You reign in the earth, let our praises unto You reign and ring out into all the earth that You are worthy to be praise. Bless Your name great God that You are in the land! We love You forever! Praise, glory, and honor be unto You! In Jesus' name we pray. Amen.

Sister Deborah Hudson
The Church at Riverside
Belcamp, MD

My Personal Prayer for God's Reign in the Earth

Dear Father,

_____

_____

_____

_____

_____

_____

_____

_____

_____

_____

_____

_____

Inspirational Thought:

"The LORD reigns! He is clothed in majesty; the LORD is clothed, and He is girded with strength. Indeed, the world is well established, and cannot be shaken." Psalm 93:1.

Prayer for a Sound Mind

"For God hath not given us the spirit of fear; but of power, and of love, and of a sound mind"

2 Timothy 1:7

Gracious Savior, Father God, our King and Redeemer, we come before Your divine presence with hearts of thanksgiving. We glorify and magnify Your Holy and righteous name. Thank You for giving us life and showering us with Your grace and mercies that are new each and every day.

Father God, we thank You for Your Word! Your Word tells us that if we call upon Your name, You would hear our cry. God, we cry out to You to touch our minds and to keep them covered in Jesus name. Oftentimes, we find ourselves emotional, and plagued with incoherent thoughts, fear, and stressors that war against our minds. We humbly come before Your throne praying for Your help. God, we pray for a sound mind of love and power. Holy Spirit, please intercede on our behalf. Help us to pray this day!

Father, we pray You will regulate our minds and direct our thoughts. Help us not to be consumed in our thoughts by the problems and calamities of this world. But Lord, help us to guard our minds, focusing our attention on those things that are true, honest, just, pure, lovely, and good. Let our thoughts be on things above and not on things beneath. Help us to understand that we are in this world, but not of this world. Father, remind us that this world is not our home, and so we should not become so wearied by the perilous times we live in. We should not become so overwhelmed by the trials and tribulations that we must face. Please put a shield around our minds, even as we put on the helmet of salvation to safeguard us from the terrors by night and the arrows by day. Let our minds not be so immersed in what is going on around us. But help us to think on Your goodness and Your loving kindness because You are faithful to us.

We proclaim that because of Your faithfulness towards us, we are daunting and unafraid—not shaken, not moved, and not faint of heart or mind. Dear God, we stand on Your Word. You did not give us a spirit of fear, but of love, power, and a sound mind. We do not accept the torment of fear in our minds. We have the Holy Ghost, Your Dunamis power working on the inside of us! Remind us as we go through the course of our day and through life situations, You did not give us fear, depression, sadness, unforgiveness or hate. You gave us so much more and so much better—a sound mind with good thoughts. Glory hallelujah! Tear down everything in our minds that is not like You. We do not want to operate out of our own thoughts and intrinsic mindsets. Uproot it all! Let the mind that is in Christ be also in us. We want our mind to be exemplary of how You would want us to think and behave. We want a sound mind with love and power!

Now God, for those times we tried to think on our own, without consulting the mind of God and the wisdom of God, please forgive us. We see how we left ourselves wide open for the enemy to get into our thoughts and steer us in the wrong direction. Thank You God for making us aware of Satan's devices. He is a defeated foe. He has no rule or reign over our thought process any longer. We relinquish our minds over to You Lord, for when You guide our minds, You guide our thoughts, and then our actions, and then ultimately our destiny. So, we place Satan in his rightful place. Not in our minds, but under our feet and render him powerless! We refuse to be double minded, wavering and unstable in all our ways. God, we command every ungodly spirit to cease from troubling and infiltrating our thoughts. We take our authority now! We bind up every confusing thought, every fearful thought, every wicked thought, and every thought that is not like You. We loose Your Word and Your Spirit over our minds.

Father God, we thank You for ministering to our minds letting us know through Your Word that You have a plan for our lives. We declare our minds are sane, rational, and rely totally on Your plan. We therefore declare, "Not my will Lord, but let Your will be done." We come into agreement with You and Your plan. Father, we pray for a heart and a mind that will move in concert with Your Spirit. We pray for a sound mind to hear Your Word, see Your works, walk in Your way, and trust in Your will. Our souls are still, our emotions are calm, and our minds are at ease. We take comfort and solace being in Your will. Our thoughts trouble us, but Your thoughts bring us calm and assurance. We declare and decree that our minds are healed, healthy, and whole. Our minds are sound. In the name of Jesus, we pray. Be glorified! Amen.

Dr. Senobia Ellis
The House of Prayer Everywhere
Decatur, GA

My Personal Prayer for a Sound Mind

Dear Father,

_____

_____

_____

_____

_____

_____

_____

_____

_____

_____

_____

_____

Inspirational Thought:

Breathe in. Breathe out. Breathe in. Breathe out. The Lord has you!
Let your mind be at ease. "*Cast all your cares upon Him because He
cares for you.*" 1Peter 5:7.

Deliverance from the Spirit of Fear

"And the peace of God, which passeth all understanding, shall keep your hearts and minds through Christ Jesus..."
Philippians 4:7

Dear Savior, I come before Your throne of grace petitioning You for deliverance—deliverance from the spirit of fear and the heavy weight it carries. Many times, I am afraid that the worse thing imaginable will happen. I panic, become so frightened, and traumatized. I want it all to stop! I do not want to be afraid, so I call out to You. Help me! The fear has taken root in me. Father, I am asking for You to teach me to be fearless and to help me trust You more in every circumstance.

Lord in those times that I feel afraid, fearing the worst or becoming consumed with worry dwelling on the "What ifs," Lord be my help. Remove my fears and worries. 2 Timothy 1:7 lets me know You have not given me the spirit of fear, but You have given me a Spirit of power, love, and a sound mind. So, I pray for Your help against this tormenting spirit. Lord, let Your Word empower me and help me to hold onto what You said I can have—a sound mind, with love and power. Please remove every doubt and fear that I struggle with and stabilize my thoughts. You, oh Lord, are a mind regulator. Help me to place my thoughts on You and not on the things I fear—*false evidence appearing real*.

God, I believe You have given me the ability to conquer all my fears through Your Word which tells me to cast all of my cares upon You because You care for me. Lord, I am casting my cares upon You. I am asking that You give me a greater capacity of faith to overcome the fear I live with each day. God, I know I need not worry or be afraid because You care for me. You are the strength of my life and the hope of all that I am. But, I still need Your help to confidently walk in that truth without wavering. Help me when I am still engulfed with fear. Take it away and bring to my remembrance Your mercies and loving kindness that keep me each day. Lord, it is because of Your mercies and love that we are not consumed. You have brought me through every situation in my life. Lord, when my heart is overwhelmed, Your mercies and love will lead me to the Rock that is higher than I. You are my great deliverer. You are my song, as the psalmist declares, *"The Lord is my strength and song..."* (Psalms 118:14)

Lord, thank You for taking away the fear and anxiousness of my soul. Thank You for taking away my restless days and sleepless nights. I will not worry over matters I cannot control. I declare that today I walk in patience to wait on You to fix matters concerning my life. I will not be compulsive with my thoughts. But, I will take comfort in knowing that Your grace and mercy, they do cover me. I call my mind to rest, knowing that You will take care of everyone of my needs, working things out for my good. Your Word tells me, *"Be anxious for nothing, but in everything, by prayer and petition, with thanksgiving, present your requests to God."* (Philippians 4:6). Father, help me not to be anxious, worried, or fearful of anything. I exchange the spirit of anxiousness and fear for Your Spirit of peace. I receive it now in Jesus name.

Now Father, I pray concerning the fear of rejection. Father, I do not want to be afraid of being rejected by those that I love. In times past, I have been rejected and made to feel unworthy of love by those I love. Because of this, sometimes I am afraid to love again. Help me Father. I want to freely give love and freely receive it. Even if my love is not reciprocated, I still want to love as You have loved me. Your love for me is unconditional. Let my love be unconditional and greater than my fears, for there is no fear in love.

Father God, I receive Your love. Keep me under the shadow of Your wings. Let Your love saturate the atmosphere of my very being so that there will be no fear, only the love of the Father. I thank You dear Lord, and praise You forever. Amen.

Sister Myrtle Williams
Christian Life Church
Baltimore, MD

My Personal Prayer
Deliverance from the Spirit of Fear

Dear Father,

_____

_____

_____

_____

_____

_____

_____

_____

_____

_____

_____

Inspirational Thought:

Be not dismayed whatever betides you. God will take care of you. May your fears fade away as you put your total trust and faith in the Lord.

Authority over Fear

"Have I not commanded you? Be strong and of good courage; do not be afraid, nor be dismayed, for the LORD your God is with you wherever you go."
Joshua 1:9

Father God, I want to thank You for Your covenant of love towards Your people. Your love is from everlasting to everlasting. It never fails. I give You praise!

Father, I come before You in the mighty name of Jesus praying against the spirit of fear. Father God, thank You there is no reason for me to fret or to be anxious about anything. I am blessed in my going out and in my coming in, in my uprising, and in my down sitting. For You are with me wherever I go! Why should I fear? You have given Your people dominion in the earth! You said in Your Word that we have power to tread on serpents and scorpions, and over all the power of the enemy and nothing shall by any means hurt us. Lord I receive Your Word. I trust Your Word that declares, *"No weapon that is formed against thee shall prosper; and every tongue that shall rise against thee in judgment thou shalt condemn. This is the heritage of the servants of the LORD, and their righteousness is of Me, saith the LORD."* (Isaiah 54:17). Lord, I thank You that no weapon that the enemy forms again me is going to prosper and that I walk in Your righteousness. Therefore, I can take my authority over that enemy called fear. I loose the Spirit of strength, courage, and might so that I can put a demand on fear with the authority You have given me.

In the mighty name of Jesus, I bind you spirit of fear. You stop your attacks against me! I condemn you and denounce you. You have no part or right to me! You are rejected, denied, refused, and defeated! The Lord God has redeemed me from your hands. I do not receive you. I am a daughter of the Most High God! That makes me a royal citizen of heaven. I sit in heavenly places in Christ Jesus. I walk in the strength of Jesus and in the power of His might. I have the mind of Christ. I know the truth and the truth makes me free from you! The blessing of the Lord is upon me! Therefore, I declare in the mighty name of Jesus that you are under my feet!

Father God, *"...teach [my] hands to war and [my] fingers to fight."* (Psalm 144:1). Every time that spirit of fear shows his ugly head, I will cut it off with Your Word! I am going to hurl Your Word at its head! *"For the Word of God is quick, and powerful, and sharper than any two-edged sword..."* (Hebrews 4:12). Thank You Father, God for Your Word. Your Word tells me, *"...greater is He that is in you, than he that is in the world."* (1 John 4:4). You made me greater than the very thing that is trying to intimidate me because You live on the inside of me. Thank You Father! Your Word says, *"Fear thou not; for I am with thee: be not dismayed; for I am thy God: I will strengthen thee; yea, I will help thee; yea, I will uphold thee with the right hand of My righteousness."* (Isaiah 41:10). God, I thank You for Your Word that helps me to fight. Your Word is exalted above my enemy. Fear must bow down to Your name!

God, You *"hath not given us the spirit of fear; but of power, and of love, and of a sound mind."* (2 Timothy 1:7). Therefore, the fear that often grips my heart does not come from You. It is of the devil!

But, I declare it is over! When Satan tries to bring intimidation and fear in my life, You will be my help Oh Lord. Satan is not Your equal or Your rival. You saw Satan fall from heaven like lightning. He was cast out of Your presence. Then, You defeated him at the cross just for me. I thank You God for casting Satan out and defeating him. Thank You Lord that You have given me power to cast Satan out of my presence and to defeat him as well, by Your power and strength! Fear has no power over me. I will not entertain it any longer, but I will give unto You LORD the glory due Your name. I will stand in victory for Your Word not only defends me, but Your blood covers me. Great are You Lord and You are greatly to be praised! Your greatness is unsearchable.

God, I thank You that from this day forth, I live in the warm embrace of Your love and not in the wet, cold, darkness of fear. I will rest in Your peace and not be worried or fearful about my past, present or future. I resist the devil and his tactics of fear, and submit myself to a loving God. I rest in Your perfect love. You are my peace and fear must flee! In Jesus' name I pray. Amen.

Sister Benita Lunn
Gods Truth Seekers
Cockeysville, MD

My Personal Prayer of Authority over Fear

Dear Father,

_____

_____

_____

_____

_____

_____

_____

_____

_____

Inspirational Thought:

Some things in life you just have to get sick and tired of and make up in your mind that you are not tolerating it anymore. That is where fear needs to be in your life, not tolerated! Turn your fears into faith by standing on God's Word and ignoring whatever Satan has to say.

Prayer against the Spirit of Confusion

"For God is not the author of confusion, but of peace, as in all churches of the saints."

1 Corinthians 14:33

Dear Heavenly Father, how excellent is Your name in all the earth. You are the God of Abraham, Isaac, and Jacob. I bow down before You as humbly as I know how, giving You honor, glory, and praise. Lord, thank You for saving me and filling me with Your Holy Spirit. I get joy when I think about all You have done for me. Lord, You give good gifts to Your children, and I thank You.

Now Lord, it is by Your Spirit that I pray against the spirit of confusion and pray for the good gift of a sound mind. God, You are not the author of confusion. You desire that we live, walk, work, and even play in peace. But, this is contrary to where we find ourselves day in and day out. Many are not living in peace, but rather living in turmoil, chaos, and confusion in their mind and in their surroundings. There is so much confusion and distress in the land. Only You are able to silence it all. You can turn the minds and hearts of many to a place of peace. Father, those that carry confusion around with them daily, creating disruptions and destruction, touch their minds so that they can exude love and kindness wherever they go. Lord, I pray even in our daily living, in our homes, on our jobs, wherever we are that there is peace, understanding, and love—but never confusion.

When confusion tries to follow us, Lord help us to resist the devil and flee from his wicked ways. Our desire Lord is to please You. So Lord, I bind up the spirit of confusion in our minds and hearts and release in us a sound mind full of gratitude and praise. Thank You, Lord for being our help. There is nothing too hard for You Lord. Help us all to draw closer to You.

God, let us have a heart's desire to get along with others and live free from contention—black and whites, democrats and republicans, husbands and wives, mothers and daughters, and fathers and sons—all dwelling in healthy relationships. Tear down the confusion that keeps us bickering, fighting, and separated from each other. Change our mindset Lord! Help us God to set our minds on things above and on our God-given purpose. For Lord, You are the Potter; we are the clay. Shape and mold our hearts and our minds. Help us to gravitate toward that which is good and peaceful, rather than that which breeds confusion, commotion and turmoil around us and within us. We do not want to be so caught up in the chaos that we miss the abundant life, the fullness of joy and the eternal life You want to give us.

Now God, I pray where there are sincere misunderstandings, mix-ups, mistakes, and misperceptions, You will come in the midst and bring clarity. Give understanding and let there be a measure of grace that we give one another in our families, on our jobs, and in our communities. Help us not to be so easily bothered, offended, or holding grudges. But God do a work within. Settle our hearts and our minds. I beseech You, Lord. Let Your ears be opened to our prayers. Arise from Your resting place and rebuke the spirit of confusion. Rebuke the spirit of confusion within us and all around us. Take total control of our minds and our situations so that we can dwell in perfect peace.

Then Lord, we pray a special payer for those with mental disorders-- those with dementia, Alzheimer's, schizophrenia, depression, anxiety, panic attacks, and other mental illnesses. Take control of their minds and war on their behalf. Quiet the storm around them. Summons Your angels to comfort them and to sing over them so that they will feel Your presence and Your peace. Administer Your healing, Lord.

God, we pray for a sound mind for all. Bring order to our minds. Align our thoughts with the perfect will of God. Thank You for clothing our mind with Your peace, joy, and wisdom. God, we lack nothing. You have given us what we need to be the slayer of confusion and to be peace makers in the earth. We thank You. In Jesus' name we pray. Amen.

Sister Marilyn I. Singletary
Solid Rock Apostolic Faith Church
Baltimore, MD

My Personal Prayer against Confusion

Dear Father,

_____

_____

_____

_____

_____

_____

_____

_____

_____

Inspirational Thought:

When there was chaos on the water, and the tempest was raging
and the sea billows rolling, the Lord simply said, _"Peace be still."_
Mark 4:39. I speak that to the confusion and chaos in your life and in
your mind, "Peace be still!"

Financial Blessings

"One who is faithful in a very little is also faithful in much, and one who is dishonest in a very little is also dishonest in much. If then you have not been faithful in the unrighteous wealth, who will entrust to you the true riches? And if you have not been faithful in that which is another's, who will give you that which is your own? No servant can serve two masters, for either he will hate the one and love the other, or he will be devoted to the one and despise the other. You cannot serve God and money."
Luke 16:10 -13

Spirit of the living God, we acknowledge Your power, presence and majesty. As we lift up this prayer, shift our heart's posture towards You. Clean and purify our hearts that our prayers may be heard and we can hear Your voice in return.

Lord, we call You Jehovah Jireh, Our Provider. We lean on You for our provision, and we thank You that You know what we need even before we ask. You alone can meet all our needs according to Your riches in glory because You are God. You own the cattle on a thousand hills. The earth is Yours and the fullness thereof. We recognize all blessings come from You.

So dear God, as it concerns our finances, we ask that You will meet our needs. Lead us and guide us in these matters, granting us Your wisdom to get wealth and to be good stewards over the financial blessings You give us. Your Word tells us in Ecclesiastes 7:12 *"For the protection of wisdom is like the protection of money."* Let us operate wisely when receiving our financial blessings. We thank You for the gifts You have given unto us to steward over. No matter the amount, allow us to be faithful, responsible, and trustworthy servants. For the time we have on earth is only temporary. Our responsibility of stewardship surpasses our earthly stay and extends into heaven. Your Word says those who are faithful with little will have the authority over ten cities in heaven. Dear God, help us not to let Your blessing pass us by. We ask for a hunger to develop from the pits of our bellies to have discernment in making fruitful decisions. Even as it concerns our finances, focus our mind and tune our ears to hear and to know what is best for the kingdom. Let us walk in faith, being willing to give of our substance, our tithes, and our offerings, to advance the kingdom of God here on earth.

God, as we make plans on how to utilize our resources, give us wisdom. Speak to our minds and give us Your plans. Do not allow us to make investments that You have not ordained, laying foundations that You have not orchestrated. Father, order our steps and surround us with the people and resources who can help us in our financial endeavors as we seek to magnify Your kingdom agenda. God, we believe that even as we continue to invest in Your kingdom, and be good stewards over what You have given us, You will bless us exceedingly and abundantly.

God, give us the knowledge to know what we need to do when our finances grow beyond our expectations, and help us to make right connections. Show us what You would have us to do as we walk in abundance. Glory to God! Show us how to invest, how to save, and also how to give. We pray that we will have a heart to give to those who are less fortunate than ourselves. Let there be a yearning within us to give to the hungry, to the poor, and to those in need. For You said in Your Word that when we help the poor we are lending to You. Let us find great joy in being a blessing to others, knowing that we are ultimately blessing You. Let us be selfless in our giving, taking great delight in helping our brothers and sisters in their times of need.

Now God, for those who are dealing with debt, show us how to recover, what steps we need to take to get in a better financial state. Let us not take matters into our own hands, but instead, trust You to deliver us and to make us financially whole. We praise You in advance for bringing us out of financial bondage and making us a blessing instead—the lender and not the borrower, the head and not the tail.

Lastly, God help us to create a legacy for our families. A good woman or man will leave an inheritance for their children's children. We claim multigenerational wealth will be birthed from us. We claim that our lineage will serve You and follow the same principles You have given to us. We claim that the next generation will continue to build on the foundations You have helped us to create. Expand their knowledge and increase their reach. We thank You for providing and entrusting us with Your provisions. Let us always be mindful of the needs of the kingdom. We praise and bless Your name and ask all these things in Jesus' name. Amen.

Minister Alexis Lee
Channel of Grace Worship Center
Edgewood, MD

My Personal Prayer over My Finances

Dear Father,

_____

_____

_____

_____

_____

_____

_____

_____

_____

_____

_____

Inspirational Thought:

God, You are my supplier. Bless me so that I may be a blessing. Give to me so that I may give to others.

Prayer for the Church

"...upon this rock I will build my church; and the gates of hell shall not prevail against it"
Matthew 16:18

The old hymn of the church declares, *"The Church's one foundation is Jesus Christ, her Lord; she is His new creation by water and the Word. From heav'n He came and sought her To be His only bride; with His own blood He bought her, and for her life He died."*
(S. J. Stone – 1866)

Father God, we are Your church and our foundation is Jesus Christ, our Lord. We were purchased by His powerful blood. May we continue to stand with You, our Creator. May we be Your representatives in the earth for we are the ecclesia, the called out. We are called out to share the Gospel of Jesus Christ. We are called out to be a witness in the earth, to save, and to heal. We are called out to deliver those who are bound. We do it all through the proclamation of Your Word, the power of the Holy Spirit, and the love of Jesus.

Father, while the world and its systems are being turned upside down, collapsing, and crumbling, help Your church to remain standing as a pillar in our communities, letting the world know that You are still seated upon the throne. You reign and rule—King of kings and Lord of lords! We thank You God that Your church is on an unshakable foundation and Your Word declares that the gates of hell shall not prevail against it. May we, the church, be forever the light of Your countenance in every situation that rises up against us. May we be a beacon of light bringing hope and encouragement in any and every dark place throughout all the ages from generation to generation. May our pastors be blessed with a shepherd's heart, moving in compassion, and leading Your people in love. May they feed us like a shepherd feeds his sheep so that we can grow into Your holy temples.

God, You know the times are changing from generation to generation. We pray that the church, Your people, will get their zeal back for the house of God. We pray they will be excited again and take great delight in coming into Your house to worship You. God, although we thank You for the many platforms there are to deliver Your Word across the world, we recognize nothing can take the place of Your church. Let the church come back to the church where they can have sweet fellowship with You and the saints of God. Let our hearts say like David, *"I was glad when they said unto me, Let us go into the house of the LORD."* (Psalm 122:1). And, while we are there in the Lord's house, let us holdfast to the taught and preached Word of God. Let the Word dwell in our hearts richly leading us to repentance and a God wisdom to walk in alignment with Your will and Your way. God, we are the church. You be formed in us, "The Hope of Glory."

God as Your ecclesia, Your church, the called out, let us be fully immersed in the culture of Your kingdom, rather than being conformed to this world. Let us be easily identifiable to the world as the daughters of God. Let us show forth Your praise and Your glory. May our hearts be full of thanksgiving and praise, not just behind the four walls of the church, but even in the market place. Keep praises on our lips so the world will see that we are Your people, the church of the living God. Let your church arise! Let Your church arise above every challenge and every spirit of darkness in our world. Let the church strive to become more like Jesus Who is the head of the church, the Rock on which we stand.

God, help us to stay on the wall contending for the faith, coming against every scheme and plan of the enemy who wants to divide and conquer the church with false doctrine, contention, and ungodliness. Let us stand in solidarity and in faith, not being moved with every wind of doctrine. May we always remember that God's Word is true and is authoritative over all. May we, the church, endure as Your unblemished bride throughout the ages, clear in our mission and our purpose. Let us walk in love and be the light and the salt of the earth. Let us stand on this truth that there is one Lord, one faith, and one baptism. Let us stand as the church, and stand with the church. You are our sure foundation on which we stand. We stand on You! Our feet are planted on the Rock of our salvation, the Rock of Ages, the Chief Corner Stone of the Church Who the builders rejected!

Father, let Your Holy Spirit permeate the church until Christ is formed in us. May we never lose our power of influence in the world. May we keep the Word of truth as a guide, "... *till we all come to the unity of the faith and of the knowledge of the Son of God, to a perfect man, to the measure of the stature of the fullness of Christ!"* (Ephesians 4:13). Father, we give You praise! In Jesus' name, amen!

Minister Andrewnetta Brown
Love Center Ministry
Tracy, CA

My Personal Prayer for the Church

Dear Father,

_____

_____

_____

_____

_____

_____

_____

_____

_____

_____

Inspirational Thought:

Do not scrutinize the church, bash the church, laugh at the church, or even leave the church. Rather, pray for God's church and love it as Jesus has loved you and even now sits on the right hand side of the Father making intercession for you. God, we thank You for Your church. So glorious to behold!

Prayer for the Burdened

"Come unto Me, all ye that labour and are heavy laden, and I will give you rest. Take My yoke upon you, and learn of Me; for I am meek and lowly in heart: and ye shall find rest unto your souls. For My yoke is easy, and My burden is light."

Matthew 11:28-30

Heavenly Father, we thank You for promising to be our great Burden Bearer! And in that spirit of knowing Who You are, we come to You laying our burdens at Your feet. As we focus on Your Word and Your promises, we submit any and everything unto You that has us feeling bound, wrapped up, and smothered. We know that when the heaviness comes, it is time to spend time with You and not run from You. Lord, You desire to exchange our ashes for Your answers, our problems for Your peace, our cares for Your calm, and our burdens for Your blessings! Have Your way oh Lord!

Dear God, in You we know we are strong; but still, You never intended for us to carry our burdens. So today, with our hearts aligned with Yours, we place all of our burdens and cares into Your capable hands. We lay in Your hands all the issues surrounding our families, relationships, finances, and our health. We give to You Lord those things that bother and burden our conscious and unconscious minds. We give to You the burden of fear-based illusions, the burden of regrets, the burden of unforgiveness, and the burden of worry. We can no longer carry these weights. They are too heavy for us to bear. Lord, just as You removed the burden of slavery from off of the children of Israel and freed them from Pharaoh and the Egyptians, free us! Help us! Break chains from off our lives! God, that same power You gave Jesus when He conquered Satan is the same power we need to conquer our enemy that is trying to keep us oppressed. Free us from every one of his tactics and attacks. Hear our prayer, oh Lord.

Almighty God, El Shaddai, there is nothing too hard for You. There is no burden to heavy that You cannot lift. We confidently put our trust in You—not man, science or medicine. We give You those burdens we carry during the day and that weigh us down during the night. We give You those burdens that try to consume our thoughts and ultimately impede our progress. We give them to You, Lord. Thank You for Your Holy Spirit Who ministers to us and gives us sweet victory over every care, every weight, and every burden. Thank You God for helping us to know You are here and we do not have to be burdened by the cares of this life. We can have peaceful days and restful nights.

Then God, thank You for Your Word which emphatically teaches us not to worry for it says, *"Therefore, I tell you, do not worry about your life, what you will eat or drink; or about your body, what you will wear. Is not life more than food, and the body more than clothes? Look at the birds of the air: They do not sow or reap or gather into barns—and yet your heavenly Father feeds them. Are you not much more valuable than they? Who of you by worrying can add a single hour to his life? And why do you worry about clothes? Consider how the lilies of the field grow: They do not labor or spin. Yet I tell you that not even Solomon in all his glory was adorned like one of these. If that is how God clothes the grass of* the field, which is here today and tomorrow is thrown into the furnace, will He not much more clothe you, O you of little faith?" (Luke 12:25-28). Lord, Your Word is able to set us free from the weight of worry and burdensome thoughts. Increase our faith and eradicate our fears and unbelief. Hear our prayer, oh Lord.

God, we appreciate how much You love us and how You show us everyday that You will take care of us. Because of Your love, we have survived the burdens of life! We survived a global pandemic, political upheaval, loses, and other strains and stressors of life's weighty matters. But our burdens cannot be compared to our victories! They cannot be compared to Your surplus of grace and mercies that we received each day. We command our mouths to speak nothing but victory. We stand in victory! Hear our prayer oh Lord.

Dear God as we stand in victory, not burdened but blessed, we buckle the belt of truth around our waist. The truth is that we do not ever have to be weighed down with burdens again because You, the Great Burden Bearer, has given us the victory over every weight of care. Thank You, Lord for hearing our prayers and attending to our needs. God, thank You for lifting our burdens, drying our tears, and mending our hearts. Thank You Lord that the weight is off our chests and we can breathe again. Indeed, You are our Great Burden Bearer! We bless You, in Jesus' name, amen.

Keisha P. Tatum
The Tab
Baltimore, MD

My Personal Prayer for the Burdened

Dear Father,

_____

_____

_____

_____

_____

_____

_____

_____

_____

_____

Inspirational Thought:

You have tried, but you cannot, carry that weight; and God never intended for you to carry it. Let it go! Release it into the hand of the Father. God's Word says, "Cast all your cares (worries, anxieties) on Him because He cares for you." 1 Peter 5:7

God through the Years

"Thou wilt shew me the path of life: in Thy presence is fullness of joy;
at Thy right hand there are pleasures for evermore."
Psalm 16:11

Bless the Lord O my soul and all that is within me. Bless His holy name. Abba Father, I give You glory, praise, and honor for Your grace, mercy, and unfailing love. I worship You in Spirit and in truth. Thank You for the indwelling of the Holy Spirit Who walks and talks with me, and Who leads and guides me. Thank You for protecting me from dangers seen and unseen. You have been my keeper, my protector, my provider, my all in all, and my total source and supply. Yes, I have been young and now I am old; yet I have never seen the righteous forsaken, nor his seed begging bread. Thank You Father for answering my constant prayer throughout the years.

Lord, my faith walk with You has brought me through many dangers, toils, and snares. You have given me strength. You have been my help. You have been a promise keeper and a heart fixer in my life. Thank You for keeping my life filled with faith, hope, and trust in Your sacred Word. God Your Word melts me, molds me, fills me, and refines me so that I can be used to do Your will. God You are so active in my life. I am grateful for my relationship with You. When I was sick You healed me. When I was discouraged, You encouraged me. Thank You, Lord for dreams and visions that have guided me along life's highway and have kept me from danger.

Lord, I continue to lean and depend on You and to walk with You on this journey. I will always have a song in my heart to sing to You, and a story in my mouth to tell others of the goodness of God. You have done so much for me. You have done great and marvelous things. You brought me through some trying times during the course of my life. I have made it this far because of Your love and the shed blood of my Lord and Savior Jesus Christ. Thank You for the blessed assurance I have in Jesus. I am grateful! I am grateful for the forgiveness of my sins and eternal life, and all the blessings I have inherited as a child of God. And although I am well stricken in years, I still stand upon Your promises and Your Word, always and forever.

When I look back over my life, I know that You, Lord, and the Holy Spirit took control of me, and established my walk and my purpose in God. I know You are a mighty, awesome, prayer answering God, and I pray You will help me to encourage the next generation to put their trust in You all the days of their lives. In Jesus' name. Amen!

Mother Sandra Amos Ponder
St. Andrews A.M.E. Church
Sacramento, CA

My Personal Prayer
God's Presence through the Years

Dear Father,

_____

_____

_____

_____

_____

_____

_____

_____

Inspirational Thought:

"Bless the Lord, O my soul and all that is within me, bless His Holy name. Bless the Lord, O my soul, and forget not all His benefits: Who forgives all your iniquities; Who heals all your diseases; Who redeems your life from destruction; Who crowns you with loving kindness and tender mercies." Psalm 103:1-4

Closing Prayer
Thank You Father!

"In everything give thanks; for this is the will of God concerning you
in Christ Jesus"
1 Thessalonians 5:18

Dear heavenly Father, we thank You for being a prayer answering God. Thank You that we can bring all our cares to You because You care for us. Thank You for being a listening ear for us individually and collectively as we call upon Your name. You care about us and You are in touch with our cares and concerns, our pain and infirmities, and our situations and dilemmas. Thank You Father!

Thank You for being the help and the strength of Your daughters. We are confident that You will hear everyone of our prayers and make things better. We believe and we receive better health, better marriages, better living conditions, better finances, better mindsets, better churches, and so much more. We, the women of God, have prayed and do continue to pray because we believe our prayers are the catalyst for fostering a change in our lives, in our families, and in our communities.

Thank You, Lord for the call to pray. Thank You for bringing us into a posture of prayer. What an honor to talk to the Father, and to make intercession for others. Thank You, Lord for giving us a heart and mind to pray. And, thank You God for helping us to pray through the precious Holy Spirit Who makes utterances for us. Thank You for supplying all of our needs according to Your riches in glory. Thank You, Lord for granting us the desires of our hearts. Thank You, Lord for directing our path, leading us and guiding us in all our endeavors.

God, thank You that things are turning around and we shall see the goodness of God in the land of the living. This is our hope and we put our trust completely in You. We pray, we yield, and watch to see what the Lord will do. Thank You Father. In Jesus' mighty name, we pray. Amen!

Dr. Dana Elaine
Dana Elaine Ministries
Baltimore, MD

My Sisters' Prayers to Our Father
Devotional

Dana Elaine Ministries

Email: info@danaelaineministries.com

Website: www.danaelainesministries.com

Made in the USA
Columbia, SC
08 February 2025

53532295R00109